Malcolm J. Hernes
598 Angell
Providence

47 Stephen Hopkins Ct
Providence, RI 02906-4309

re - re - re - re - re - re - re - read

17 June 2004
[ Malikzade ] 7 FB

24 February 2003

[ Malikzade IV ] D 22

Re - read
7 march 2003
[ Malikzade V ] X 7

# OF NO COUNTRY I KNOW

re - re - re - re - re
re - re - read

2 august 2004
[ Malikzade IV ] E 12

re - re - read
19 april 2003
[ Malikzade VI ] D 8

117 East Manning St.
Providence, R.I. 02906 - 4309

[ St. Columba ] re - read
re - re - re
9 June 2003
[ Malikzade IX ] D 12

The publication of this book was supported by
a grant from the Eric Mathieu King Fund
of The Academy of American Poets

# re - re - re - re - read
27 June 2003
[ Malikzade X ] D 7

re - re - re - re - re - read
3 november 2003
[ Malikzade XI ] D 19

PHOENIX **POETS**

A SERIES EDITED BY ALAN SHAPIRO

**DAVID FERRY**

# of no country I know

*New and Selected Poems and Translations*

THE UNIVERSITY OF CHICAGO PRESS
*Chicago and London*

The University of Chicago Press, Chicago 60637
The University of Chicago Press, Ltd., London
© 1999 by The University of Chicago
All rights reserved. Published 1999
Printed in the United States of America

08 07 06 05 04 03 02 01 00    2 3 4 5

ISBN 0-226-24486-5 (cloth)
     0-226-24487-3 (paper)


Title page illustration: Detail from a Roman mosaic representing the Epicurean
philosophy.


Library of Congress Cataloging-in-Publication Data


Ferry, David.
     Of no country I know : new and selected poems and translations /
David Ferry.
         p.   cm.—(Phoenix poets)
     Chiefly poetry in English; some selections from Horace and Virgil translated
from Latin into English.
     Includes bibliographical references.
     ISBN 0-226-24486-5 (alk. paper).—ISBN 0-226-24487-3 (pbk.: alk.paper)
     1. Latin poetry—Translations into English.   2. Rome—Poetry.
     I. Title.   II. Series.
     PS3556.E77037   1999
     811'.54—dc21                                        99-20899
                                                              CIP

*For Anne*

Of love and truth with long continuance,
　　　Let others learn from what my love has taught me;
All you who study how to turn away
　　　From the governance of love, come learn from me
All that the course of faithful love has brought me,
　　　Than whom there never was whose heart was surer
Of what it knows and holds, since I first saw her.

Neither for joy, nor sharp adversity,
　　　Nor for disdain, dread, danger, or despair,
For life, for death, for woe, for destiny,
　　　For bliss, for bale, for comfort, or for care,
For chance of fortune, turning here and there,
　　　From her shall never turn my plain heart true,
Whatever I suffer of sorrow, old or new.

My married heart shall never turn from her
　　　Unto another so long as my five wits
Shall last, whose whole consent is given to her
　　　Until death's rage shall cleave me to the root.
So I shall love her ever, in spite of what-
　　　Soever circumstance can do to us.
God grant I go to the grave before she goes.

　　　　　[—adapted from the Bannatyne Manuscript]

*And for Stephen, Elizabeth, and David*

# Contents

STRANGERS: A BOOK OF POEMS (1983)

*from* GILGAMESH: A NEW RENDERING IN ENGLISH VERSE
(1992)

# *Foreword*

The extraordinary power, depth, elegance, and astounding originality of David Ferry's poetry are nowhere more subtly yet conspicuously on display than in "Down by the River," one of the new poems in his *Of No Country I Know: New and Selected Poems and Translations.* "Down by the River" is a sort of urban, postmodern pastoral, in which the poet describes and celebrates a June day along the Charles River in Cambridge:

The page is green. Like water words are drifting
Across the notebook page on a day in June
Of irresistible good weather. Everything's easy.

On this side of the river, on a bench near the water,
A young man is peaceably stroking the arm of a girl.
He is dreaming of eating a peach. Somebody's rowing,

Somebody's running over the bridge that goes over
The highway beyond the river. The river is blue,
The river is moving along, taking it easy.

A breeze has come up, and somewhere a dog is barking,
Acknowledging the stirring of the breeze.
Nobody knows whose dog. The river is moving,

The boats are moving with it or else against it.
People beside the river are watching the boats.
Along the pathway on this side of the river

Somebody's running, looking good in the sunshine,
Everything going along with everything else,
Moving along in participial rhythm,

Flowing, enjoying, taking its own sweet time.
On the other side of the river somebody else,
A man or a woman, is painting the scene I'm part of.

A brilliantly clear diminutive figure works
At a tiny easel, and as a result my soul
Lives on forever in somebody's heavenly picture.

   The scene he celebrates in language, and the language itself, or the act of
writing itself, are interwoven: the page, like the water, is green; and also like the
water the words he uses to describe it are "drifting" across the green notebook
page. Everything, he says toward the end of the poem, is "moving along in par-
ticipial rhythm." Inside and outside, mind and nature, language and world,
dream and reality, animal and human, agree with one another, and yet because
everything is in motion the agreement, the poem implies, is ephemeral. The on-
ward participial flow of the syntax stands in tension with or is balanced by the
stability of the lines themselves, a stability created by the coincidence of line and
phrase, so that the stasis of art enacted by the lines and the motion of time en-
acted by the coursing sentences are simultaneously apprehended.
   The great surprise of the poem, however, comes in the closing lines:

On the other side of the river somebody else,
A man or a woman, is painting the scene I'm part of.

A brilliantly clear diminutive figure works
At a tiny easel, and as a result my soul
Lives on forever in somebody's heavenly picture.

If in the architectural firmness of its lines and in its clarity of image, the poem feels deeply informed by the classical past, it also turns that past on its head. The value of monumentality in art, the Horatian confidence of perpetuating one's mortal identity in immortal art, is reversed here, for it isn't the poet who has made the monument but the tiny figure who, by painting an image of the poet, has preserved his soul. That wonderfully unexpected, modest yet I think profound gesture conveys Ferry's sense both of isolation and community, of solitude and society, and of transcendence as momentary and communal, ordinary and transient, and of art as both an acknowledgment of time and a resistance to it.

I've gone on at length about this seemingly unambitious poem because it demonstrates the delicate yet ferocious power of Ferry's work. He is both one of the most traditional poets in America and one of the most experimental. There is no poet writing in English today who surpasses the beautiful precision of his verse; its rhythms, made perceptible by the measure, enact his emotional and intellectual perceptions, unfailingly providing effects of fine awareness. He writes in a wide variety of forms with astonishing mastery; and as his prosody responds to the variety of demands made upon it, his imagination responds by becoming more inclusive and unpredictable.

More generally, the special power of his work, early and late, depends on his ability to negotiate between the claims of a deeply lyrical imagination and a deeply skeptical intelligence. His poems provide a moving record of what it feels like to inhabit a world where there are no certain dwelling places. It is a world of bewildering effects whose causes are always elsewhere and unknown, or known, at best, only enough to make us intensely aware of what escapes our knowing. His abiding concern is mortality, the fragilities of the flesh, and the precarious nature of the bonds that constitute our selves as individuals, as spouses, parents, friends, and citizens. This sense of estrangement, desire for connection, and of life as a perpetual wandering tempered only by love and empathy is reflected in the titles of each collection—*On the Way to the Island, Strangers, Dwelling Places*—and in the title of this volume of selected poems, *Of No Country I Know*. But while the preoccupations remain the same, the poems themselves—and the translations that participate with them in this lifelong enterprise—change in wholly unexpected and surprising ways. It isn't quite right to describe this changefulness as an evolving maturity. Maturity is way too smug or sober or conventional a term to account for the freedom and flexibility and even radical innocence Ferry attains. One feels, reading his work, poems and translations alike, a continual and cumulative opening out of possibility. He is one of those rare poets who seems, as we read this poetry working out its concerns, to grow younger and wiser at the same time. He is a great poet and this is a great book.

Alan Shapiro

# Acknowledgments

The following new works were previously published in the following publications:

*Agni:* "Eclogue Nine"
*Harvard Magazine:* "Down by the River," "Wallenda" (September—October 1996)
*Journal of the Association of Literary Scholars and Critics:* "Eclogue Five"
*New Republic:* "Courtesy"
*Provincetown Arts:* "At Lake Hopatcong"
*Raritan:* "An Autumn Afternoon," "Character of Mary in Earlier Life," "Movie Star Peter at the Supper for Street People," "News from Mount Amiata," "What's Playing Tonight"
*Slate:* "That Evening at Dinner" (© 1997 Microsoft Corporation)
*Threepenny Review:* "The Chair"
*TriQuarterly:* "She Speaks Across the Years"

The poem printed as an epigraph to "On a Poem by Arthur R. Gold" is one of "Three Fragments: Things That Last," in Arthur R. Gold's *Poems Written During a Period of Sickness* (Somerville, MA: Firefly Press, 1989). Reprinted by permission.

The excerpts from *Gilgamesh: A New Rendering in English Poetry* (© 1992), *The Odes of Horace: A Translation* (© 1998), and *The Eclogues of Virgil: A Translation* (© 1999) are reprinted here with the kind permission of Farrar, Straus & Giroux, Inc.

NEW POEMS AND TRANSLATIONS

I

# What's Playing Tonight

Not twenty feet away were the walls of the house next door
     Where Bradley's mad mother and Bradley's sane father lived.

The shagbark hickory tree, absurdly tall, loomed over
     The little houses at night, their house and ours.

A movie kept on playing across the street on the screen
     That was the front of the house over there asleep.

She didn't know how to stop the movie projector so
     She didn't know how to change the movie ever.

It played the same movie over and over again in the night.
     Pictures of dead Bradley still alive.

The neighborhood glowed with the flickering light of the silver screen
     That Bradley's mother's movie was playing on.

# Character Analysis of Mary in Earlier Life

Her spinster eccentricity often
Said things for the sake of startling you.

She was like that. It seemed a form of shyness,
Putting you off with her charm flirtatiously.

It was a powerful entrapped wild innocent conventional nature.

The rage in her charm steadily
Burned its way through the materials of her life

So that there was always almost nothing left.
To put it another way:

Where she was was always stranded on a high platform
She got to on high heels getting across

On a tight rope strung out over the abyss.

# At Lake Hopatcong

A picture taken years before I was born:
My mother, her sister Sis Nellie, their mother,
Whose name was Emma Saunders Russell, holding

My sister Eleanor, a babe in arms,
My father in a stiff high collar and a boater.
My mother is smiling, her hand on her hip. She's wearing

A brimless hat (is it a toque?) with a high dark
Upstanding feather. Sis Nellie and my mother
Are standing sideways to the car, their faces

Turned to the camera, so that together they frame
The icon of my grandmother and my sister.
I recognize from later memories

Sis Nellie's stylish intelligent-looking face,
The elegant round gold glasses. She is wearing
A tweed coat of some relatively light color,

And a hat with a narrow brim but full above,
Gathered by a silver buckle to a peak.
My mother's wearing a dark coat with an open collar,

Showing the white blouse over a dark skirt.
The blouse has dark buttons. The family group
Is standing in front of a high auto with tall

Thin wheels, with gracile tires and wooden spokes,
And a canvas top, a beautiful grill adorned
By a radiator cap that looks like a saltcellar.

There is a fluent decoration painted
As if incised on the surface of the hood,
Of the kind that you still can see, painted on trucks,

That gives them their incongruous feminine charm
And delicacy, as if the figuration
Was music playing across the metal surface.

The canvas roof of the car's like a little tent
Or pavilion someone put up to celebrate
Their Sunday outing in New Jersey, in nineteen-

Sixteen. Probably the picture is being taken
By Uncle Frank, Frank Stanley, Sis Nellie's husband.
Because of the limits of the camera

The sky is hard to read. Impossible to tell
The time of year on that weekend afternoon.
I think I can read in her witty-looking face,

From what a doctor told us many years later,
Some things about Nellie's subsequent life which she
Was already concealing and concealed her whole life long,

Her lifelong unbroken hymen, and I therefore know
Some things she didn't know about yet, or was only
Part way through knowing about, in all the story

Of that future, the frustrated sexuality turned
Into malice abetted and invigorated
By the cultural verve and ignorance of the place

And circumstance in which she was brought up,
At Willoughby Spit, near Ocean View, at Norfolk.
But in my grandmother's face there's little to read,

Because I know little about her, so I take her
Almost "as she is," a pleasantfaced woman,
Obviously with trouble with her teeth,

As seen by the conformation of her mouth,
Smiling without opening her lips. All I know of her
Is that my mother said she was sweetnatured

And full of equanimity; my sister's
Memories of her in my sister's early childhood
Seem to confirm this. And I know that my grandmother,

As a young girl, was given away to others,
From one family with many children
To another, cousins, or friends, kissing kin,

With none. Saunders is I guess the family name
She was given into. My father looks "handsome and youthful."
His shoes are brightly shining, and he's wearing

A dark vest and a vestchain under his coat.
I'm puzzled about the straw hat that he's wearing,
Since the women's coats (my grandmother's also wearing

A heavylooking coat, black, like her hat,
Because she was widowed just a few years before)
Look heavy, wintry, or at least autumnal.

The trees look thinly leaved, as if it were
Late autumn, early spring, or winter in a place
Where dead leaves cling to trees all winter long.

You cannot tell what weather or season it is.
My mother, as in all these early pictures,
Although in this one already having lost

Her girlish slimness, looks sexually alive,
Full of energy, her hair dark, abundant,
Her smile generous (though maybe less so than

In the pictures taken a few years earlier).
Somewhere in this picture there is inscribed
The source or secret, somewhere inscribed the cause,

Of the anxious motherly torment of disapproval,
The torment not resisted by my father,
Visited by my mother on my sister,

The baby in the picture, torment that was
Perhaps in turn the cause of the alcoholism
That, many years later, the baby in the picture

Won out over. But it's all unreadable
In this charming family photograph which, somehow,
Perhaps because of the blankness of the sky,

Looks Russian, foreign, of no country I know.

# *Wolf Woman*

When I look into my mirror
I see that my two eyes

Are different from each other.
One of them scares the other.

This eye that scares is darker.
You can't see to the bottom

Where there are thoughts, maybe,
At the bottom of the pool,

The pool of eyesight where
The seeing comes up from.

The scared eye tries to look
Away from the other eye.

It pulls to look away,
But the other eye won't let it.

Its look follows the other.
Anguish is my prey.

# Little Vietnam Futurist Poem

She came into my view as vivid as
Somebody on a screen in a movie seen,
Elegant in the focus of my eye.

Birdboned. Quick and light. Not wearing pajamas.
The little run resembling playfulness.
Calling out something, screaming something or other

As if her little mouth was fervently singing,
As if you couldn't hear what the words could be,
Because of the singing. I had her in my sight.

Other people were there, wearing pajamas,
Streaming out of some hideyhole or other
Into the way that that was how I saw them.

The trees of the kind that grew there establish the place.
We know that way the story of what it was.

# Song of the Drunkard

—*Rilke*

I don't know what it was I wanted to hold onto.
I kept losing it and I didn't know what it was
Except I wanted to hold onto it. The drink kept it in,
So at least for awhile it felt as if I had it,
Whatever it was. But it was the drink that had it
And held it and had hold of me too. Asshole.

Now I'm a card in the drink's hand while he keeps smiling
Like he doesn't give a shit in a game that's going badly,
And when death wins he'll scratch his scabby neck
With the greasy card and throw me down on the table
And then I'll just be another one of the cards
In the pile on the fucking table. So what the fuck.

## Movie Star Peter at the Supper for Street People

The style a form of concealment the way style is.
His manners seemed a parody, almost,
Of manners, a movie star of bygone days;

Strangely elaborate, highly stylized manners,
Complicit with his fame and with your praise;
Looking toward you and then away from you,

Star-like, movie-star-like, a dance routine,
The walk almost a glide, or elegant shuffle,
Always on the verge of veering away,

Circling away and over to the other side
Of the frozen skating arena that he was on;
A dancer's courtesy, the courtesy,

I mean, of the dancer to the audience,
Flirtatious and familiar, only for you,
And entirely impersonal and withheld.

All of the above, though, maybe, misses the point,
Because it seems to say he knew about
What he was doing or what the style was for,

And nothing let one be sure that this was so;
A look on his face of amusement, as if he knew
A secret that he shared with you and yet

Kept to himself, as if it only showed
The cryptogram but wouldn't provide the key
To read it with. But could he read the code?

One night, late at night, as we were driving
Home from having had dinner out, in Boston,
We saw him figure skating through Charles Street Circle,

Right through and among the circling lights of cars
As if with champion skill on thin ice whirling
Oblivious to the astonished blaring horns,

As a dancer or skater seems, while dancing to
The music that we hear, oblivious to
The music that we hear and listening to

Some other music heard from somewhere else.
So Peter moved like a dancer or skater through
And among the dangerous outraged cars as if

Untouchable and untouched and moving to
The sounds of something else from somewhere else—
The music maybe of his madness was it?

It was as if he skated in solitude
And glided whirling on a lonely tarn
Far out away from everything there is.

# On a Poem by Arthur R. Gold

> *Do you*
> *Remember slow-moving trolleys?*
> *Do you remember men dropping*
> *From the rear-end platforms*
> *Of slow-moving trolleys?*
> *So our faith in God slowly*
> *Drops but not the monkey*
> *On our backs, not his nails*
> *Digging into our necks:*
> *Guilt, justice, the desire*
> *To be good.*
> *Is There No End?*
>
> —Arthur R. Gold

God, lights flashing, bells ringing, God on his tracks,
Heading away somewhere, to some destination.

Who were the people who managed to get on board?
Where is it they were being taken to?

Arthur, yes, I remember the slow-moving trolleys;
I remember the men clinging on to the trolleys,

Clinging like monkeys not just to rear-end platforms
But hanging on by their nails just under the cables

That hooked up above to the flashing sparking lines.
A lot of fireworks, God, on your way to some station,

Rattling and clanging, making a lot of noise.
One thing you're famous for is making noise.

Then, suddenly, in the poem, God is the monkey
That rides us like the habit we can't get free of,

And for Arthur in his extremity not being able
To free himself from virtue was part of the pain;

The obligations of being what he was,
Father, and teacher, setting some kind of example.

My sister Penny at my niece's house,
The day her blood reported that the cancer

Had intensified ten times since the last report.
The obligation of being who she was,

Listening to the family pleasantries
With something like what seemed to be like pleasure.

# *Wallenda*

I saw him in a coffeeshop in Cambridge,
Radiant, argumentative, talking away
As joyful as anything, terrified, dying,
Sisyphus in a panic, the words pushing
The joy ahead of him like a stone up hill;
Or else he was like a bicycle racer racing,
Faster and faster racing what he was saying,
Because in what he was saying no matter what,
He couldn't get out ahead of the sniggering voice
He kept on hearing whispering under his talking,
Telling him what was going to happen to him;
Or else he was standing out on the edge of a cliff
Trying his best to shout into the wind
That was blowing hard in against him from the planets;
Or else he was "carrying a twenty-three-foot
Balancing-pole and he moved out smoothly onto
The three-quarters-of-an-inch-thick cable one-
Hundred-and-twenty-feet high, beginning his
Seven-hundred-and-fifty-foot walk. The weather was bright
Cold and windy. He continued to move out smoothly
Until he reached the midpoint. Then suddenly
The wind picked up to thirty miles per hour.
He leaned into the wind to lean against it.
The wire was 'dancing' now under his feet.

'Sit down, sit down,' one of his family called.
He semi-crouched and called out down to the nine
Men who were working the guy wires down below,
'Tighten it, tighten it.' DAREDEVIL. Then he tried
To grab the cable but could not hold it and then
Put both hands back on the pole and silently
Daredevil Wallenda fell plummeting down to death."

# Backyard Dog

Out in the winter moonlight,

Out in the cold snow,

The dog is running around,

Around and around and around

In the fenced-in backyard,

In spirals ignited by

The binocular's wondering gaze,

Magical dogtracks out

In the cold winter moonlight,

The dogtracks spiraling

Around and around, a soul,

A saying, a writing being

Written over and over,

Written and rewritten

In the newly fallen snow.

# The License Plate

On the way back from the hospital we saw
A message on the license plate of a car.

It said GOD HAS. Has what?
Decided finally what to do about it?

The answer to the question that you asked?
The whole world in His Hands? Fucked up? Again?

Apologized? Failed to apologize?
The car went on its way ahead of us.

# An Alphabet

ABC
You and me

DEF
Dumb and deaf

GHI
Blind of eye

JKL
What's to tell?

MNO
All you know

PQR
Who you are

STU
Who are you?

VWX
Stones and sticks

YZ
You and me

**II**

# My Harvest

—from "Mein Eigentum," Hölderlin

The autumn day is quiet in its fullness.
The grapes are ripe, and the hedges red with berries;
Already many beautiful blossoms have fallen
Gratefully down to the earth to be received.

And as I make my way along the path
I see how men are laboring in contentment
Over there in the fields, because their work
Has ripened into a harvest of good fortune.

# An Autumn Afternoon

The rich fume of autumn rises from the ground
In light and odor as the leaves rot marvelously

In the hot autumn sun in the brilliant afternoon.
What was green is turning to light before my eyes.

The hawthorn leaves have not yet fallen away.
The squirrels are fat. The winter is coming soon.

There's something frantic in birdflight. The shadows of wings
Print and unprint erratically on the little

Porch roof that I look out on from my window,
As if to keep taking back what has just been said.

# Courtesy

It is an afternoon toward the end of August:
Autumnal weather, cool following on,
And riding in, after the heat of summer,
Into the empty afternoon shade and light,

The shade full of light without any thickness at all;
You can see right through and right down into the depth
Of the light and shade of the afternoon; there isn't
Any weight of the summer pressing down.

In the backyard of the house next door there's a kid,
Maybe eleven or twelve, and a young man,
Visitors at the house whom I don't know,
The house in which the sound of some kind of party,

Perhaps even a wedding, is going on.
Somehow you can tell from the tone of their voices
That they don't know each other very well—
Two guests at the party, one of them, maybe,

A friend of the bride or groom, the other the son
Or the younger brother, maybe, of somebody there.
A couple of blocks away the wash of traffic
Dimly sounds, as if we were near the ocean.

They're shooting baskets, amiably and mildly.
The noise of the basketball, though startlingly louder
Than the voices of the two of them as they play,
Is peaceable as can be, something like meter.

The earnest voice of the kid, girlish and manly,
And the voice of the young man, carefully playing the game
Of having a grown-up conversation with him:
I can tell the young man is teaching the boy by example,

The easy way he dribbles the ball and passes it
Back with a single gesture of wrist to make it
Easy for the kid to be in synch;
Giving and taking, perfectly understood.

# Down by the River

The page is green. Like water words are drifting
Across the notebook page on a day in June
Of irresistible good weather. Everything's easy.

On this side of the river, on a bench near the water,
A young man is peaceably stroking the arm of a girl.
He is dreaming of eating a peach. Somebody's rowing,

Somebody's running over the bridge that goes over
The highway beyond the river. The river is blue,
The river is moving along, taking it easy.

A breeze has come up, and somewhere a dog is barking,
Acknowledging the stirring of the breeze.
Nobody knows whose dog. The river is moving,

The boats are moving with it or else against it.
People beside the river are watching the boats.
Along the pathway on this side of the river

Somebody's running, looking good in the sunshine,
Everything going along with everything else,
Moving along in participial rhythm,

Flowing, enjoying, taking its own sweet time.
On the other side of the river somebody else,
A man or a woman, is painting the scene I'm part of.

A brilliantly clear diminutive figure works
At a tiny easel, and as a result my soul
Lives on forever in somebody's heavenly picture.

# Hälfte Des Lebens

*—Hölderlin*

The yellow pear tree boughs
And the wild-rose branches hanging
Over the quiet waters;
And the swans, a little drunken,
Kiss, and kiss again,
The sacred summer waters.

Alas, when winter comes,
Where will I find such flowers?
Where will I find the sunlight
And shadows of the summer?
The walls are speechless, cold;
The weather vane bangs in the wind.

# An die Parzen

*—Hölderlin*

Give me, O You who have the power to do so,
But one summer more, and the autumn following after,
To bring my songs to harvest. And then my heart,
Satisfied with its playing, may willingly die.

The soul that never finished the work for which
It came into this world will never rest easy
Down there with Orcus; but if the work gets done,
Then I will unprotestingly go down

Into the stillness of the world of shadows.
What if I cannot carry my lyre with me?—
One time, at least, I lived as the gods live.
Nothing more than this was necessary.

# Roman Elegy X

*—Goethe*

Alexander, Caesar, Henry, Frederick the Great—
    There isn't one who wouldn't give me half
Of what he got being great if he could have
    One single night of what we have together.

Poor things, now Orcus has them in his power.
    You who are living, lovers, revel in pleasure
In love's warm bed before your horrified foot
    All of a sudden recoils from Lethe's touch.

# News from Mount Amiata

—*Montale*

By later tonight the fireworks of the storm
Will be a swarming of bees below the horizon.
I'm writing this letter to you at a wooden table
Whose wood the insects and worms have gotten into.
The beams are pockmarked with their ravenous feasting.
A smell of melon mildew rises from the floor,
As from the valley rises the valley smoke,
As it were the smoke of mushrooms, clouding my window.
Here in the rich core of the world, in this room,
In this honeycomb, mealy, fragrant, innermost cell
Of a sphere launched out across the luminous skies,
You who are elsewhere and other dwell in another
Cell and center of things, but, here at this table,
Writing to you, in front of this fire the chestnuts
Lavishly burst themselves open upon the hearth of,
That life is too brief that invokes your absent presence
Against the glowing background as of an icon.

Outside the windows the rain is falling . . .

If you
Were to make your way among the ancient feeble
Soot-blackened buildings time has made that way,
And along the alleys between them, and through the courtyards
Where in the middle there is a wellhead where
The well goes down forever and forever,
If you could follow the heavy flights of nightbirds
Down the alleys to where, beyond the ravine,
The galaxy glimmers, the matrix of our torment . . .
But the only step that echoes along the darkness
Is that of someone by himself who sees
Shadows of doorways falling, shadows collapsing;
The threads between the stars are lost to sight;
The clock in the campanile is stopped at two;
Even the vines that climb the ancient walls
Are shadows that climb in the dark.

North Wind, come down,
Unloosen the hands that clutch the sandstone walls;
Scatter the books of hours on the attic floors.
Clear all away, cold wind, and then, let all
Be clearness of sight that has dominion over
The mind that does not know how to despair.
Cold wind, seal up the spores from which the tendrils
Sprout that then climb as shadows the ancient walls.
These alleys are too narrow; the donkey hooves
That clatter in the darkness on the cobbles
Strike sparks the unseen mountain peak above
Replies to with magnesium random signals;
And oh the leaking slowly deliquescing
Walls of the huddled houses in the rain,
Time turning to water, the endless dialogue
With the wretched dead, the ashes, oh, the wind,
The death, the death that lives. . . .

This Christian fuss—
Nothing but words of shadow and of grief—
What can I say through them that speaks to you?
Less than the water draining away down the runnels.
An old abandoned mill wheel, the trunk of a tree,
Markers of the limits of the world . . .
A pile of litter shakes and disintegrates . . .
At night the porcupines come out, seeking
A trickle of water to pity them . . . They join
My waking vigil to your deep dreaming sleep.

# About Sylvia's Stories and Teaching

What's being taught
Is how language is seeing,
Telling, exacting.

And how we're caught
In language: in being,
In feeling, in acting.

# She Speaks Across the Years

*—Hölderlin*

"If having gone so far from one another
On distant ways, if across all the ways
And all the time, you know me still who was
Your partner in those days in all the sorrow,
Then something after all is left of it all.

Where's she who loved you waiting for you now?—
Here in the Civic Garden, just as before,
Here where in memory once again we're meeting,
In the dusk, as before, and after all the sorrow,
Beside the flowing black original river.

There were those moments, I remember there were those moments,
When you, so closed up in yourself, were able,
With me, to be, if, just for a moment, less so.
There was something good about that, for you, for me.
The time went by as if there was no trouble.

I remember how you showed me all those places
That though this was my country I had never
Visited or seen as through your eyes,

The open fields, and also the hidden places
Looking from concealment out over the sea.

Was it in springtime then? Was it in summer?
The nightingales and the other birds were singing
And the fragrance of the trees was all around us;
And the hyacinth, the violets, the tulips,
Green ivy on the housewalls, green the shadows

Of the pathways where we walked together then,
Thinking it all, after all, was possible.
It wasn't that you were different than you were,
Nor I than I, but that we were for awhile
All right together in our separate selves . . ."

# *That Evening at Dinner*

By the last few times we saw her it was clear
That things were different. When you tried to help her
Get out of the car or get from the car to the door
Or across the apartment house hall to the elevator
There was a new sense of heaviness
Or of inertia in the body. It wasn't
That she was less willing to be helped to walk
But that the walking itself had become less willing.
Maybe the stupid demogorgon blind
Recalcitrance of body, resentful of the laws
Of mind and spirit, was getting its own back now,
Or maybe a new and subtle, alien,
Intelligence of body was obedient now
To other laws: "Weight is the measure of
The force with which a body is drawn downward
To the center of the earth"; "Inertia is
The tendency of a body to resist
Proceeding to its fate in any way
Other than that determined for itself."

That evening, at the Bromells' apartment, after
She had been carried up through the rational structure
By articulate stages, floor after flashing floor,
And after we helped her get across the hall,

And get across the room to a chair, somehow
We got her seated in a chair that was placed
A little too far away from the nearest table,
At the edge of the abyss, and there she sat,
Exposed, her body the object of our attention—
The heaviness of it, the helpless graceless leg,
The thick stocking, the leg brace, the medical shoe.

At work between herself and us there was
A new principle of social awkwardness
And skillfulness required of each of us.
Our tones of voice in this easy conversation
Were instruments of marvelous finesse,
Measuring and maintaining with exactitude
"The fact or condition of the difference
There was between us, both in space and time."

Her smiling made her look as if she had
Just then tasted something delicious, the charm
Her courtesy attributed to her friends.

This decent elegant fellow human being
Was seated in virtue, character, disability,
Behind her the order of the ranged bookshelves,
The windows monitored by Venetian blinds—
"These can be raised or lowered; numerous slats,
Horizontally arranged, and parallel,
Which can be tilted so as to admit
Precisely the desired light or air."

We were all her friends, Maggie, and Bill, and Anne,
And I, and the nice Boston Brahmin elderly man
Named Duncan, utterly friendly and benign.

And of course it wasn't whether or not the world
Was benign but whether it looked at her too much.
She wasn't "painfully shy" but just the same
I wouldn't be surprised if there had been
Painfulness in her shyness earlier on,
Say at dancing school. Like others, though, she had
Survived her childhood somehow. Nor do I mean
She was unhappy. Maybe more or less so
Before her marriage. One had the sense of trips
Arranged, committees, concerts, baffled courage
Living it through, giving it order and style.
And one had the sense of the late marriage as of
Two bafflements inventing the sense they made
Together. The marriage seemed, to the outside world,
And probably was, radiant and triumphant,
And I think that one could almost certainly say
That during the last, heroic, phase of things,
After his death, and after the stroke, she had
By force of character and careful management,
Maintained a certain degree of happiness.

The books there on the bookshelves told their stories,
Line after line, all of them evenly spaced,
And spaces between the words. You could fall through the spaces.
In one of the books Dr. Johnson told the story:
"In the scale of being, wherever it begins,
Or ends, there are chasms infinitely deep;
Infinite vacuities . . . For surely,
Nothing can so disturb the passions, or
Perplex the intellects of man so much,
As the disruption of this union with
Visible nature, separation from all
That has delighted or engaged him, a change

Not only of the place but of the manner
Of his being, an entrance into a state
Not simply which he knows not, but perhaps
A state he has not faculties to know."

The dinner was delicious, fresh greens, and reds,
And yellows, produce of the season due,
And fish from the nearby sea; and there were also
Ashes to be eaten, and dirt to drink.

# Multas per gentes

—Catullus

O my poor brother, I have journeyed here,
    Through many foreign lands and many seas,
To come to this unhappy ceremony,
    Seeking to speak to ashes, that cannot speak,
Since Fortune has taken you yourself away—
    Alas, my brother, cruelly taken you.

According to the custom of our fathers
    I bring these offerings for the wretched dead.
Accept, my brother, what I have brought you, weeping.
    *Ave,* forever *vale,* my poor brother.

# *Shubshi-meshre-Shakkan*

*—Babylonian*

HYMN

I sing this hymn in praise of him who is
The wisest of all, raging in darkness, or,
In the bright morning, calm, the wisest of all.

The storm of his anger it is that lays the land low;
His breath in the quiet morning stirs but a leaf;
The flood of his anger cannot be withstood.

He is the lord who pities and forgives.
The sky will buckle under the weight of his hands;
He holds the sick man gently in his hands.

The thorns of his whip cut into the flesh and it bleeds;
His poultice cools and eases the body's pain;
It eases the pain and the wounded body heals.

He has but to frown and the strength departs from a man;
The strength departs from a man and the man is weak.
The Lady Fortune departs, seeking out others.

He smiles and the personal god comes back to the man,
His strength comes back to the man and re-enters his body.
The Lady Fortune returns from where she had gone to.


NARRATIVE

*i*

Everywhere around me there is confusion.
Enlil and the other gods have given me up.

The personal god has gone away from my house.
The Lady Fortune has gone to somebody else.

I see the omens everywhere I look.
The king, the sun that shines on his happy people,

The king is angry and he will not hear me.
When I go to the palace now, they look at me.

One person blinks and another looks away.
What are these omens? How is it I should read them?

When I lie down to dream I have nightmares.
In the street I see the others looking at me.

I see how people point their fingers at me.
I hear them talking about me in the street.

One says: "I made him want to end his life,"
One says: "I will take over his position,

I'll be the one who goes and lives in his house . . . "
Six or seven talking in the street,

Six or seven gathered in the street,
Storm demons raging against me in the street.

*

The year has turned and everywhere I see
Wherever I look the signs of my bad luck.

I cannot find out anywhere what is right.
I pray to my personal god and he doesn't answer.

I pray to the Lady Fortune, she will not listen.
I went to the dream interpreter, he poured

Libations to the gods but they said nothing.
The *zaqiqu* spirit said nothing; nothing was what

Could be done by the one whose charms can charm away
The evil spirits. Everywhere around me

There is confusion. Everything is strange.

*

It is as if I did not pray to the gods.
It is as if I did not properly say

The name of the goddess before I eat my meal.
It is as if I did not teach my household

How to honor the gods. It is as if
I taught my household people how to neglect

The holy days and festivals of the year.
I kept the rules; to worship was my joy;

The music of the procession delighted me;
Before I ate I spoke the name of my god;

I taught my people how to honor the gods,
And to honor the king as if he were a god.

I taught my people how to respect the palace.
I wish I knew these things would please the gods.

I wish I knew the meaning of these things.
Who knows the will of the gods in heaven? Who knows?

Maybe the gods despise what men think right.
Maybe what men think wrong delights the gods.

Who knows the ways of the gods of the Underworld?
What man has ever learned the ways of the gods?

Today he is dead who was living yesterday;
From gladness to sorrow is but the blink of an eye;

He sings in joy this moment who wails the next.

*ii*

Around me everywhere there is confusion.
Everything is strange. A storm wind drives me along.

Sickness has come upon me. An evil wind
Has blown in from the horizon. As new little plants

Come up through the ground in spring when their time has come,
The Weakness comes up through the ground. The Coughing comes up,

It comes up horribly laughing out of the abyss.
The Headache comes up out of the Underworld.

The Bone-Ache comes from the surface of the waters.
The *Lamashtu*-demon comes down from the mountain.

All of the demons gather themselves upon me.
The phlegm fills up my throat and my throat chokes.

Whatever I eat is vile. Beer, solace of men,
Is vile in my mouth. Grain is vile in my mouth.

All night the demons torment me. What are they saying?
I cannot hear what it is that they are saying.

Where has my dignity gone, and my good looks?
The exorcist has nothing to say. The diviner

Has nothing to say. My personal god has not
Come to my rescue. The Lady Fortune has not.

My chest was broad, my arms were strong, and now
A boy could easily wrestle me to the ground.

My looks are strange. The flesh is loose on my bones.
I try to walk. My feet have forgotten how.

My knees are fettered and bound like the busu-bird's.
At night I lie in my shit like an ox or a sheep.

My grave is open already and waiting. Already
All the funeral things have been prepared.

He who gloats gloats when he hears about it.
She who gloats gloats when she hears about it.

The day is dark for all my family.
For all my friends lamenting the day is dark.

*iii*

His hand was heavy upon me, I could not bear
The weight of his hand, I could not bear the fear

Of the storm wind screaming against me and blowing against me.
I lay awake or else I was asleep.

There was a young man, beautiful, wearing new garments.
I dreamed a priest was holding in his hand

A bough of tamarisk that purifies.
There was a young woman came to me in my dream,

Beautiful, wearing new garments. She spoke to me:
"Here is deliverance from your wretchedness."

There was a young man came to me in my dream,
Bearded, wearing a headdress. He carried a tablet

And on the tablet written was a message:
"Marduk has sent me. I come to bring you luck.

To Shubshi-meshre-Shakkan I bring good luck."
The storm of Marduk's anger was quieted down.

A lion was eating me. Marduk muzzled the lion.
Marduk took my hand and raised me up.

He who had thrown me down he raised me up.
My knees, which were fettered and bound like the busu-bird's,

My knees were freed from their bonds and I could walk.

My throat, which was closed, was opened, and I sang.

HYMN

The Babylonians saw what Marduk had done
And everything they said proclaimed his greatness,
The storm of his anger it is that lays the land low;

His breath in the quiet morning stirs but a leaf;
The flood of his anger cannot be withstood.
He is the lord who pities and forgives.

Who would have thought this man would see the sun?
Who would have thought this man would walk again?
Who would have thought we would see him on the street?

What god but Marduk could bring back the dying?
Who would have thought this man would see the sun?
Who would have thought we would see him on the street?

As far as the land extends and the sky above it,
Wherever the sun god shines and the fire burns,
Wherever the waters are and where the winds blow,

Wherever the creatures are whom the goddess Aruru
Fashioned of clay, endowed with breath and life,
The black-headed creatures, men, who walk the earth,

Let there be praise for Marduk for what he has done.

# Old People

Their old skin has the marks in it of the sea.
The patterns of waves. Traces of sand crabs in the patterns.
Wind traces. Splinters of seashells. Markings of kelpfronds.

Their voices are loud against the waves coming in.
They shout out into the wind that blows back into
Their mouths the words they are trying to shout out into

The wind that blows against them. What they possess
They possess with a fierceness that comes from a deafness that isn't
Deaf, but it hears the waves say take them, take them.

But they cry out against the waves in voices
Violent and weak I won't give in to them.
They're in a room full of people almost without

Any furniture only some metal chairs,
So the walls resound and Cerberus barks a lot.
It is a nightmare of the high school lunchroom.

# *Janus*

*—adapted from Ovid, Fasti*, I, 95–120

My house filled up with light in the midnight dark.
The headlights swiveled against me, swiveled and yawed.

It was the old—two-headed—god looking at me.
My hair stood up on end. Cold terror froze my chest.

Noise and confusion. "Chaos was my name
When the ancients named me. There was a time when earth,

Air, fire, and water were clotted together, all
One inchoate lump; and then they four

In discord separated, one from the other.
Fire went up higher than all the others,

Air intervened between the fire above
And the earth below, and the sea was below the earth,

Each of them in its place, although uneasy.
All things are what I govern, just at that moment

When out of nothing they turn into something.
I Janus am the ore and residue."

# First Night

A stump. A post. An effigy not made
As yet. A toe. A toe in the icy waters.

A door that's open just a little.
What's that in the next room?

What flows underneath our house?
*Timor mortis conturbat me.*

*

First night. Absence of light. Presence
Of cold. Numb fingers play the instruments.

Down in the street a little horn is tooting.
Cold fog in the throat.

Trying to clear the throat, a new beginning.
*Timor mortis conturbat me.*

*

The year turns over heavily in its sleep.
The whole sky wheels above the starry treetop

That is the sleeping city's dreaming head.
If I should die before I wake

I pray the Lord my soul to take.
*Timor mortis conturbat me.*

# The Chair

The chair left out in the garden night all winter
Sits waiting for the summer day all night.

The insides of the metal arms are frozen.
Over the house the night sky wheels and turns

All winter long even behind the day.

*from* ON THE WAY TO THE ISLAND (1960)

# The Late-Hour Poem

In an hour of furious clarity,
By liquor made,

Full of a fierce charity,
My harp I played.

I made a loud uproar!
I went in turn

From door to every door.
Marry or burn!

Love your neighbor, I cried.
Pity the poor

Divided people, who side
By side here lie,

Transfixed in sleep; and shadow
Covers each eye!

On house and house the echo
Rang and rebounded.

My harp made everybody know
How brave I sounded!

# The Bird

Minding of itself, and mildly, in its finding,
And modestly, submissive to the weather—

Storm, wind, the bird's peril—this bird I saw
That did not see me in my human body watching;

Watchful the bird was only of itself,
And listening to itself, with softliest mutter,

And twitter, and quietest fluttering of feather,
Attentive to the minutiae of its task.

# The Soldier

Saturday afternoon. The barracks is almost empty.
The soldiers are almost all on overnight pass.
There is only me, writing this letter to you,
And one other soldier, down at the end of the room,
And a spider, that hangs by the thread of his guts,
His tenacious and delicate guts, Swift's spider,
All self-regard, or else all privacy.
The dust drifts in the sunlight around him, as currents
Lie in lazy, drifting schools in the vast sea.
In his little sea the spider lowers himself
Out of his depth. He is his own diving bell,
Though he cannot see well. He observes no fish,
And sees no wonderful things. His unseeing guts
Are his only hold on the world outside himself.
I love you, and miss you, and I find you hard to imagine.
Down at the end of the room, the other soldier
Is getting ready, I guess, to go out on pass.
He is shining his boots. He sits on the edge of his bunk,
Private, submissive, and heedful of himself,
And, bending over himself, he is his own nest.
The slightest sound he makes is of his being.
He is his mother, and nest, wife, brother, and father.
His boots are bright already, yet still he rubs

And rubs till, brighter still, they are his mirror,
And in this mirror he observes, I guess,
His own submissiveness. He is far from home.

# At a Bar

While in a bar I bore
Indignity with those
Others whose hearts were sore
Or sour or sick or such
As made them humankind,
I looked into my glass
To see if I could find
Something to give me ease.

Narcissus at the pool,
I looked lovingly at
My own disordered fool,
Who would not tell me much,
But stared patiently back.
He would not tell me what
I'd ever have or lack.
He would not tell me that.

I looked along the bar
And saw my fellow creature
Bravely standing there.
*By word, sign, or touch,*
I cried in my mute heart,
*Tell me, be my teacher,*

*Be learnèd in that art,*
*What is my name and nature?*

My pulse ticked in my wrist;
The noon hung around unawares;
Outside the traffic passed.
Like quiet cattle or such,
Standing about a pool,
Dumb, ignorant creatures,
My fellow, my self, my fool,
Ignorant of our natures.

# Out in the Cold

The sun shines in the ice of my country
As my smile glitters in the mirror of my devotion.
Flat is the scene there. There are a few scrub bushes.
I live on the edge of the land. The frozen sea
Lies locked for a thousand miles to the North, to the Pole.

Meager my mouth, and my knuckles sharp and white.
They will hurt when I hit. I fish for a fish
So thin and sharp in the tooth as to suit my malice.
It stares like any fish. But it knows a lot,
Knows what I know. Astonishment it has not.

I have a hut to which I go at night.
Sometimes there is no night, and the midnight sun
And I sit up all night and fish for that fish.
We huddle over the ice, the two of us.

# A Farewell

Let the day fall like light out of the eye.
Out of the ear let its music go. From the touch
Let the touching of air retire. Remain in the dark,
Dumbly remain in the dark. What will they know
Of you then, or want, when, then, in the dark you remain?

Knowledge began with the pressure of light on the eye,
And the ear spun out of thin air its airy tune.
Let no vein flutter or flicker to signal the blood's
All but imperceptible errand. Does the skin
Shudder or shiver at all at least conjunction?

Shrink, then, into your dark, be locked up in yourself,
Shadow of shadow be in your nothing dark,
Oh be keep to yourself, be close, be moat, be wall
All dark. Hush. Hear hush. Vanish. Know nothing.
How then will the day light knock at the lid in vain!

# In the Dark

I wandered in my mind as in the dark.
I stumbled over a chair, ran into a wall,
Or another wall, I wandered down a hall,
And into another room, the same as before.
I stumbled against a wall, I felt the floor
Carefully with each foot, I found a door,
And into another room, the same as before.
I wandered in my mind, I was in the dark.
I sidled up against another wall,
I shouldered along it, searching for a door,
And found one, opening out into a hall
That led to another room, the same as before.
In fear I tuned my voice to a little tune,
A crazy tune that sang inside my head,
And followed the tune as one would follow a thread
That leads one to or from a minotaur.
And that tune led me back or forward mazily,
That sang inside my head so crazily!

I followed or fled at last into a hall
That had a little light. Down at the end
Of the hall, a long way off, two windows were,
And into the windows came a little light.
I followed down the hall as to a friend

Long since offended. Timidly I wore
An anxious smile, eager to please. The light
Grew brighter still, till at last to the end
Of the hall I came. What a wonderful sight!
I found that I was looking through my eyes!
Outside of myself what a beautiful landscape lies!

# Learning from History

They said, my saints, my slogan-sayers sang,
Be good, my child, in spite of all alarm.

They stood, my fathers, tall in a row and said,
Be good, be brave, you shall not come to harm.

I heard them in my sleep and muttering dream,
And murmuring cried, How shall I wake to this?

They said, my poets, singers of my song,
We cannot tell, since all we tell you is

But history, we speak but of the dead.
And of the dead they said such history

(Their beards were blazing with the truth of it)
As made of much of me a mystery.

**II**

# *Augury*

Beautiful alien light, the lovers lie
In trouble in the park, whose summer leaves
Obstruct their sight of what's been shaped for them
In icy configurations of the stars.

# The Embarkation for Cythera

The picnic-goers beautified themselves
And then set sail for Cythera, with jugs
To keep their coffee hot, martinis cold,
And hampers full of music. The water shone
For them that day, and like a street of jewels
Lay between their land and the island.

Their cockle hull was pretty, white and gold
As the Mozarteum, and their laughter picked
Its way, nicely as tunes of proper jump,
From port to starboard, gentlemen to ladies
And return. They played their cards right, whiling
The day away by smiling and by thinking

Of the times to come, the banquets in the grove
On the antless island of that ancient idol
Love, the girl who rose to be the pearl
To deck them out. Thinking of her, each lady
Fingered her necklace, and sweet music tattled
From the spinet of her desire; each lord

Touched at his sleeve for the ace he'd hidden there.

# On the Way to the Island

After we fled away from the shuddering dock,
The sea upheld us, would not let us go

Nor drown us, and we danced all night in the dark,
Till we woke to discover the deck was made of glass,

All glass, and, leaning together, we lovers looked down,
Say a hundred miles, say a million years, and there

Were the fish, huge, gaping, motionless, flashing
Their innocent frightening scales in the dark!

# Quand vous serez bien vieille

—*Ronsard*

When you are very old, at night, by candlelight,
Sitting up close to the fire, unwinding or winding the thread,
Marveling you will murmur, telling over the songs of the dead,
"Ronsard praised this body before it became this fright."

Not one of your companions, dozing over her spinning,
But, hearing you say these things in her old woman's dream,
Will be startled half-awake to bless your famous name
For the praise it had deserved of my immortal singing.

I will be under the earth, my body nothing at all,
Taking its rest at last, under the dark myrtle;
There you'll be by the fire, a hunched-up old woman

That held off my love for a long look in the mirror.
Listen to what I say, don't wait for tomorrow:
These flowers in their blossom go quickly out of season.

# The Crippled Girl, The Rose

It was as if a flower bloomed as if
Its muttering root and stem had suddenly spoken,

Uttering on the air a poem of summer,
The rose the utterance of its root and stem.

Thus her beautiful face, the crippled girl's,
Was like the poem spoken by her body—

The richness of that face!—most generous
In what it keeps, giving in its having.

The rose reserves the sweetness that it yields,
Petal on petal, telling its own silence,

Her beauty saying from its thorny stalk
That what it is is kept as it is given.

# Musings of Mind and Body

*the mind*

      I am that thing the sea cast up, a shell
      Within whose murmuring round the tide or wind
      Murmur their old music. My coil is cunning,

      Envy, malice, pity, contemplation . . .
      The wave that cast me out upon this beach
      An hour ago, where I sit singing alone,

      Will lace me round with her green arms, come tide,
      Come evening, and I will be gone. Meanwhile
      I hum to myself myself in a humming dream.

*the body*

      I am that sea. What I cast up is mine,
      Whenever I choose to take it back or not.
      The driest bloom that spreads its papery petal

      Far inland bears my legend on its flowering.
      Read my sign in the lizard's grin. My voice
      Cries out in the falling flesh of the great Bathsheba.

      The little dog that leaps up in the field
      Leaps up as if to leap out of my reach.
      But I will wash him down. And thou, my mind.

# Poems of Marianne Moore

*i*

Let her look at a stone:
The stone becomes an apple,
The apple of her eye.

Nor is it only the stone:
Her eye becomes a hand
To hold the apple up,

Gently for the mind,
Which is the truest eye,
Kindly to look upon.

*ii*

To squeeze from a stone its juice,
And find how sweet it is,
Is her art's happiness.

# Johnson on Pope

*—from The Lives of the Poets*

He was protuberant behind, before;
Born beautiful, he had grown up a spider;
Stature so low, he could not sit at table
Like taller men; in middle life so feeble
He could not dress himself, nor stand upright
Without a canvas bodice; in the long night
Made servants peevish with his demands for coffee;
Trying to make his spider's legs less skinny,
He wore three pair of stockings, which a maid
Had to draw on and off; one side was contracted.
But his face was not displeasing, his eyes were vivid.

He found it very difficult to be clean
Of unappeasable malignity;
But in his eyes the shapeless vicious scene
Composed itself; of folly he made beauty.

# Dog and Fox

The quick brown fox jumps over the lazy dog.
He does indeed, and the dog, who does not doze,
Jumps after the fox and catches him in his jaws.
Pray, citizen smart, can you tell me please what cause
For enmity between such pleasant creatures?
I have looked everywhere for learnèd teachers
To latin me this: why does the lazy dog
Not *waltz* with the quick brown fox, and they together,
As true friends should, brave fair and stormy weather?

# The Unawkward Singers

Self-praise is a wonderful thing!
It causes all the birds to sing:
The sparrow's brag, thrush's conceit,
They make the whole world cheerly repeat,
Cheerly repeat their praise!

For any lark there is no other,
No father, mother, sister, brother,
No sweet wife, nor no dear love;
The dove's the pool in which the dove,
Loving, admires his ways.

Coiled from the swan's throat,
His final, operatic note:
Impassioned on himself he dies,
Knowing the world is him, is his,
By his self-celebration.

Master man cannot so please
Himself with the eloquence of these.
Thus, clumsily his song is sung,
Thick praise by a thick tongue
For its own limitation.

# *What It Does*

The sea bit,
As they said it would,
And the hill slid,
As they said it would,
And the poor dead
Nodded agog
The poor head.

O topmost lofty
Tower of Troy,
The poem apparently
Speaks with joy
Of terrible things.
Where is the pleasure
The poetry brings?

Tell if you can,
What does it make?
A city of man
That will not shake,
Or if it shake,
Shake with the splendor
Of the poem's pleasure.

**IV**

# By the Sea Shore

Now the tree
That had been stone
Is stone again:

Another age
With notice none
Of what had gone

And come again,
And every tide
Registers on

The roaring page
The change of bone
To ice, and stone

To flower, and sea.

# *The Beach at Evening*

The beach at this evening full-
Tide is a fisherman's back,

Whose bright muscles of rock
Glisten and strain as they pull

The cast net of the sea
In with a full catch

Of pebble, shell, and other
Things that belong to the sea.

# Descriptive

Alone, I looked down through the afternoon:
A long lawn, a great tree, a field, and a fountain.
The whole day was full of its colors that moved
About, above, within, and of each other,
Bodies in the blindnesses of love.
The whole day was alive with its own creating.
Nothing was still, would stay, and for a while
I looked at all this as if it were all I wanted,
Colors and shapes, fluid as one another,
So that the tree, which seemed at one moment a tree,
Seemed at another an inexhaustible fountain
Cascading about itself in a green fall
Of water that never fell, and the green lawn
Was the water that never fell, running away.

# *Aubade*

If the early morning were like the dewy steaming
Rising of cloudy brightness

Out of the shadowy gardens of this sleep;
Were like this long last night's last dream, unquenched,

Drifting from the eye's
Opening splendor on the day's first instant;

Oh if the early morning
The slight smoke were of the banked fire of the sleeping

Ardor I watched so long,
So long heard breathe in the heart of the heart's easy

Selfhood, knowing nothing but its sleeping:
Then were the morning one

Creation of your body's dear awakening.

# *Envoi*

The ancient cup of tears, the pastoral legend,

Hid in the wood from which we've long since strayed,

Is it the pool in which we cannot look now

Nor drink from the dark freshness of that source

From which the pure words sprang that could be spoken

To utter a sorrow impersonal as legend?

STRANGERS: A BOOK OF POEMS (1983)

*"Think thou how that this is not our home in this world, one not knowing another's speech and language."*

—The Diary of Samuel Ward, 13 May 1595

I

# A Tomb at Tarquinia

The two of us, on the livingroom couch,
An Etruscan couple,
Blindeyed to the new light let suddenly in;
Sitting among the things that belong to us,
The style of living familiar and easy,
Nothing yet utterly lost.

Leapers and dolphins adorn the painted walls;
The sun is rising,
Or setting, over a blue Tyrrhenian Sea;
In the pictured cup the wine brims and glistens;
An unknown flower burns with odorless incense
The still air of the place.

# At the Bus Stop; Eurydice

The old lady's face.
Who knows whose it was?
The bus slid by me.
Who in the world knows me?

She was amazed, amazed.
Can death really take me?
The bus went away.
It took the old lady away.

# Ellery Street

How much too eloquent are the songs we sing:
Nothing we tell will tell how beautiful is the body.

It does not belong
Even to him or her who lives in it.

Beautiful the snail's body which it bears
Laboriously in its way through the long garden.

The old lady who lives next door has terribly scarred legs.
She bears her body laboriously to the Laundromat.

There's a fat girl in the apartment across the street.
I can see her unhappiness in the flower she wears

In her hair; it blooms in her hair like a flower
In a garden, like a flower flowering in a dream

Dreamed all night, a night-
Blooming cereus. A boy passes by, his bare

Chest flashing like a shield in the summer air;
All-conquering,

The king going to the drug store.
The snail crosses the garden in its dignified silence.

# My Mother's Dying

I listen at the door.
Who's dying, then?
It's like bird-watching.

Who's going to die next?
Birds in the nest.
Who knows about all this?

# Several Voices

*the tall man*

> Height scares me. I am always afraid of falling.
> The snaky sea lies coiled around my feet.
> When I fall down those snakes will ravin me.

*the fat woman*

> I billow on my bones. The axle of the world
> Bears seas about itself in its difficult turning.
> Where is this heavy world lumbering to?

*the pretty girl*

> The blossom on the stem, tossed in a sunny wind.
> The hummingbird and bee come to me for favor.
> Giving and taking, we're a whole act together.

*the old sick man*

> What scares me is the bright touch of a sharp point
> Of white light, piercing my dark.
> I prayed I'd go to sleep in that pitch dark.

# A Night-Time River Road

We were driving down a road.
Where was it we were going?
Where were we driving to?
Nobody knew.

Behind the blur of trees
Along the river road,
Somewhere behind the blur
A dark river ran.

The car bore us along.
We didn't know who we were
Or where we were going to.
Somebody must know.

Somebody in the car
Must know where we were going,
Beside the dark river,
Where we were going to.

All silent in the car
We sat staring ahead.
Where were the lights of a bar,
A gas station, a house?

Out in the dark the river
Was telling itself a story.
There in the car nobody
Could tell where we were going.

**II**

# On a Sunday Morning

My child and I
Are walking around the block.
No sea heaves near. No anger
Blooms through the perfect sky.

The flashing of the wheels
Of a passing car is not
The flashing of that fate
I might have feared, not this Sunday.

A page from a newspaper
Drifts along the gutter.
It is a leaf
Fallen from a terrible tree,

The tree of anger,
Tears, fearfulness.
It is nothing to him,
And nothing to me, this Sunday.

# Sculptures by Dimitri Hadzi

This metal blooms in the dark of Rome's
Day light. Of how many deaths
Is Rome the bright flowering?
See, the dead bloom in the dark
Of the Fosse Ardeatina. The black
Breath of the war has breathed on them:
Shields gleam, and helmets, in the memory.

Their flowering is their being true
To their own nature; not being
A glory, a victory; being a record,
The way things are in war.
In the nature of things the flowers grow
With the authority of telling the truth:
Their brightness is dark with it.

# *Evening News I*

We have been there

        And seen nothing

Nothing has been there

        For us to see

In what a beautiful distance

        In the fresh dews

And morning lights

        How radiantly

In the glistening

        The village is wasted

It is by such sights

        The eye is instructed

# Evening News II

The face looking into the room;
Behind it light, shaking, like heat
Lightning; the face calm and knowing;
Seeing, but not seeing who I am;
The mouth may be telling something.

Something about our helplessness;
Something about the confusions of beasts;
The consequence of error; systems
Haywire, or working; the stars gone
All wrong in the body's courses.

Out on the plain of Mars, brilliantly
Played under the lights, searched out
Beyond any answer, the game went on
Far into the night; the bloodiest came
Home from the battle seeking the prize.

The women were disgraced; hair streaming,
Pleading into the staring: buy, buy—;
Was it my daughter I was seeing?—
The humiliation was pleasing: tears,
Laughter, smiles, all mingled together.

The light swallowed itself, a balloon
Deflating; somewhere in the darkness
A murmuring let itself go.

# Caprimulgidae

Though *Caprimulgus* can only totter or hop
A few steps at a time, almost a cripple,
Nevertheless, perhaps on the flat roof
Of some city building or out on the bare ground,
Or catlike lengthwise stretched along a limb,
It lies all day, waking in its sleeping,
Capable, safe, concealed in its cryptic plumage,
Invisible to almost anything;
Its nightready eyes are closed, carefully
Keeping the brilliant secret of its flight;
Its hunting begins when the light begins to go.

It makes its flight in the competence of its own
Way of behaving; hovering, or gliding,
Floating, oddly, just at the edges of bushes,
Just over the ground, or near the vagueness of trees,
At twilight, on the hunt for moths or other
Creatures out in the failing evening light.
It feeds while flying softly, smiling, smiling,
The gape open to far back under the ears;
In the dim air it looks like a giant moth
Fluttering, the blurred disheveled feathers waving,
Signaling something that understands its meaning.

# A Charm

I have a twin who bears my name;
Bears it about with him in shame;

Who goes a way I would not go;
Has knowledge of things I would not know;

When I was brave he was afraid;
He told the truth, I lied;

What's sweet to me tastes bitter to him;
My friends, my friends, he doesn't love them;

I walk the daylight in his dream;
He breathes the air of my nightmare.

# On Haystack Mountain

I stand here, on the top of the mountain, here
In the dark, looking out over the night's darkness
As over a dark ocean. Even by day
The ocean's a kind of darkness, with all it conceals;
So the darkness, with all it conceals, is a kind of ocean.

I look up at the night sky, picked out with all
Its famous stars, how clear, in a cold how clear
Society of love. Peacefulness, quietness,
The dark spaces between the bright stars . . .

In my unquestioning heart is some restful grief
Or pleasure, here in the dark, on the mountain,
Under the famous stars, here in my sole self,
For once not anxious or sorry, contending for now
Not at all with anger or ambition . . .

# The Waiting

Someone hammering something somewhere outside;
The sound of the plumbing faithfully dying away
Somewhere in the building; the ocean noises of cars
From blocks beyond, like the quiet breathing of waves;
The mad young woman waits for her faithful lover;
Her innocent curtains tell her the secrets of summer air.

She stands at her window and waits; somewhere outside
Someone is hammering something; the ocean is breathing;
The mailman has come and gone, he spoke her name;
The curtains whisper a little against the sill;
How often he comes to her door, the imposter, her lover;
He speaks in a secret tongue understood by no other.

# Table Talk

How can he stand it,
Being talked about that way?
His every madness the subject
Of every dinner table
Talk that's unworthy of him?

I saw his wife on the street,
Her mouth showing the pain
Of the self-discipline
His trouble imposes on her.
What is it for, all the talk?

I saw his daughter, too,
Small, ordinary, charming.
What will it be for her?
Madness cries out too loudly.
The pain is too much to bear.

*God bless unthinking living.*
*God bless this house and all*
*Those who live within it.*

# Cythera

There they go, down to the fatal ship.
They know how beautiful they are.
The ship will sail very soon. The sea
Will cover them over very soon unknowingly.

Wave goodbye from the shore, children.
I can see how your faces change in the sight
Of their going away. Wave to them.

Their sails are of silk, they're very pretty.
The sunset is all smiles, radiance.
The hues of a first, or last, innocence.
You look hungry, children, tired, angry.

Very beautiful is the manner of their going:
Music is playing about the mast; their lovely faces
Look lovelier still compared to the angry children.

## In Eden

You lie in our bed as if an orchard were over us.

You are what's fallen from those fatal boughs.

Where will we go when they send us away from here?

# A Walk in the Woods

Sweet bird, whose song, like all natural things,
Is but the saying aloud of what is withheld from me,
The knowledge of what it means,

I have known times when one who is dear to me,
Spoke to say something as lovely as what the sweet bird sings,
Alone, in a green thicket.

# Seen Through a Window

A man and a woman are sitting at a table.
It is supper time. The air is green. The walls
Are white in the green air, as rocks under water
Retain their own true color, though washed in green.
I do not know either the man or the woman,
Nor do I know whatever they know of each other.
Though washed in my eye they keep their own true color.

The man is all his own hunched strength, the body's
Self and strength, that bears, like weariness,
Itself upon itself, as a stone's weight
Bears heavily on itself to be itself.
Heavy the strength that bears the body down.
And the way he feeds is like a dreamless sleep.
The dreaming of a stone is how he feeds.

The woman's arms are plump, mottled a little
The flesh, like standing milk, and on one arm
A blue bruise, got in some household labor or other,
Flowering in the white. Her staring eye,
Like some bird's cry called from some deepest wood,
Says nothing of what it is but what it is.
Such silence is the bird's cry of the stone.

# Out at Lanesville

*—in memoriam Mary Ann, 1932–1980*

The five or six of them, sitting on the rocks
Out at Lanesville, near Gloucester; it is like
Listening to music. Several of them are teachers,
One is a psychologist, one is reading a book,
The page glares white in the summer sunlight;
Others are just sunning themselves, or just
Sitting there looking out over the water;
A couple of them seem to be talking together;
From this far off you can't hear what they are saying.

The day is hot, the absolute middle of summer.
Someone has written an obscenity
In huge letters on the rocks above and behind
This group of people, and someone else, one of them,
Maybe, or maybe a neighbor, the owner of one
Of the cottages up behind and back in the woods,
Has tried to erase it and only partly done so,
So that for years it will say hoarsely FUCK
To the random winds and to the senseless waves.

One of them is sitting with her back turned
To me and to the others on the rocks. The purple

Loosestrife and the tigerlilies are like the flags
Of some celebration; they bloom along the edge
Of a small stream that makes its way unseen
Down to the rocks and sand. Her shoulders are round,
And rather luxuriously heavy, and the whole figure
Has a youthful and graceful amplitude of being
Whose beauty will last her her whole life long.

The voices of some people out in a boat somewhere
Are carried in over the water with surprising
Force and clarity, though saying I don't know what:
Happiness; unhappiness; something about the conditions
Of all such things; work done, not done; the saving
Of the self in the intense work of its singleness,
Learning to live with it. Their lives have separate ends.
Suddenly she turns her head and seems to look
Toward me and toward the others on the rocks,

So that her body, turned away, is more expressive
Than her blank face, a pure reflector of light.

**IV**

# To Sestius

*—Horace, Odes i.4*

Now the hard winter is breaking up with the welcome coming
      Of spring and the spring winds; some fishermen,
Under a sky that looks changed, are hauling their caulked boats
      Down to the water; in the winter stables the cattle
Are restless; so is the farmer sitting in front of his fire;
      They want to be out of doors in field or pasture;
The frost is gone from the meadowgrass in the early mornings.
      Maybe, somewhere, the nymphs and graces are dancing,
Under the moon the goddess Venus and her dancers;
      Somewhere far in the depth of a cloudless sky
Vulcan is getting ready the storms of the coming summer.
      Now is the time to garland your shining hair
With myrtle and with the flowers the free-giving earth has given;
      Now is the right time to offer the kid or lamb
In sacrifice to Faunus in the firelit shadowy grove.

Revenant whitefaced Death is walking not knowing whether
      He's going to knock at a rich man's door or a poor man's.
O goodlooking fortunate Sestius, don't put your hope in the future;
      The night is falling; the shades are gathering around;
The walls of Pluto's shadowy house are closing you in.
      There who will be lord of the feast? What will it matter,

What will it matter there, whether you fell in love
     With Lycidas, this or that girl with him, or he with her?

# La Farandola dei Fanciulli

—*Montale*

How far back the ancient past seems now.
Those kids dancing around and playing,
By the railroad track, up back of the beach,
On the gravel and cinders of the railbed,

Weeds suddenly breaking into blossom
In the heat of the day, a flowering of thirst.
It's as if being naked and nameless
Was being sunlight, flower, heat-shimmer.

# In Balance

—*Jorge Guillén*

I am so happy. It is wonderful
To breathe the air and be in the morning light.
On a day like this, if the soul weighs anything
It is like the weight of a flower bending itself
Down to the earth in the weightless light and air.

Everything calmly gives itself up
To happiness on a day like this. The whiteness
Of a wall gives whiteness to the eye that looks at it.
The grass in the vacant lot across the street
Yields to the morning breeze that flows across it,

Till the breeze dies down like the end of a sentence spoken.

v

# *A Telephone Call*

A strong smell of dog, of my dog's death;
My old dog is lying there, giving me lessons in dying.

I talked to my father, my father called me tonight:
The sour breath of the telephone telling the truth.

# At the Hospital

How beautiful she had become:
Strange fish,
In that aquarium;

A rare find,
She swam in that element,
In the body's knowledge.

# At the Hospital

As with the soft authority of wings
Obscurely rustling, angels, we, or else
Expressionless as policemen, in our clothes,
Carefully unaccusing brought the word
Of health and gladness as we passed along
The shining hospital corridor in the brilliant
Frightening Sixties to the final place
Where on her wretched bed my sister Betts
Lay dying at the bottom of her room.

Above her head, on the television screen,
Endlessly dying on the hotel floor,
Lay Bobby Kennedy as about him danced
The dance of consternation flittering out
Along the echoing channels of the night.

# To Sally

Now we've been sitting up all night,
Waiting to find out
What the story is.

I watch your beautiful patient face;
It's as if you didn't know
All that you know.

Your mother in mortal danger, you speak
Of something funny that happened.
What will have happened,

Maybe, before your story's finished?
Good people are punished
Like all the rest.

# At the Hospital

She was the sentence the cancer spoke at last,
Its blurred grammar finally clarified.

**VI**

# After Spotsylvania Court House

I read the brown sentences of my great-grandfather,
As if—not even as if, but actually—
Looking into a brown photograph as old
As his writing is. In his sentences
Two innocent naked young men, Methodists,
Bathe in the morning in the Rapahannock River,
At Fredericksburg, Virginia, eighteen sixty-four.
*Brother Pierson and I went out and bathed in the Rapahannock.*
*Returned to take our breakfast on coffee and bread.*
I can see the young men bathing in those sentences,
And taking their breakfast, in the letter home.
*We sat down on the clean grass, in the Garden;*
*Around us strawberries, cherries, gooseberries, currants*
*Were ripening, though not yet ready for use . . . .*

An unluxurious incense, intense, dry, pure,
Rises from this letter and from his life.
*The morning air seemed to take up the song of our praise.*
*It is a wonderful honor to be here and to do good.*
The river is flowing past the hospital,
*Nearly as wide as the Delaware at Trenton,*
*And like it shallow.* I can see the young men walking
Through the early streets, on the way to the hospital,

*With paper and jellies and clothing, all laden down.*
The morning vapor is rising from the river.
*There were about 200, some of them so young.*
*We wrote letters for them, bound up wounds, prepared*
*Delicacies. We prayed, and sang "A Charge to Keep."*
The incense has the odor of old paper.

# Photographs from a Book: Six Poems

*i*

A poem again, of several parts, each having to do
With a photograph. The first, by Eakins, is of his student,
Samuel C. Murray, about twenty-five years old,

Naked, a life study, in the cold light and hungry
Shadow of Eakins's studio in Philadelphia.
The picture was taken in eighteen ninety-two.

The young man's face is unsmiling, shy, or appears to be so
Because of the shadow. One knows from other
Images in the book that Murray's unshadowed gaze

Can look out clear, untroubled, without mystery or guile.
His body is easy in its selfhood, in its self and strength;
The virtue of its perfection is only of its moment

In the light and shadow. In the stillness of the photograph
I cannot see the light and shadow moving
As light and shadow move in the moving of a river.

He stands against what looks like the other side
Of a free-standing bookcase, with a black cloth
Draped over it, and a shelf as the top of it,

And on the shelf, sad, some bits and pieces
Of old "fine" culture and bric-a-brac:
An urn; a child's head; a carved animal

Of some sort, a dog or a wolf, it's hard to tell;
A bust of a goddess staring out at nothing;
Something floral made of wood or plaster.

"The Arcadians inhabited the earth
Before the birth of Jupiter; their tribe
Was older than the moon. Not as yet

Enhanced by discipline or manners, their life
Resembled that of beasts; they were an uncouth
People, who were still ignorant of art."

*iii*

There is a strange, solemn, silent, graceless
Gaiety in their dancing, the dancing of the young
Ladies of Philadelphia in the anxious

Saffron light of Eakins's photograph;
There in the nineteenth century, dressed in their "Grecian"
Long white dresses, so many years ago,

They are dancing or standing still before the camera,
Selfhood altered to an alien poetry,
The flowers in their hair already fading;

Persephone, Dryope, Lotis, or maybe only
Some general Philadelphia notion of Grecian
Nymph or maiden, posing, there by the river.

"If those who suffer are to be believed,
I swear by the gods my fate is undeserved."
The light in Eakins's photograph is ancient.

*iv*

Plate 134. By Eakins. "A cowboy in the West.
An unidentified man at the Badger Company Ranch."
His hat, his gun, his gloves, his chair, his place

In the sun. He sits with his feet in a dried-up pool
Of sunlight. His face is the face of a hero
Who has read nothing at all about heroes.

He is without splendor, utterly without
The amazement of self that glorifies Achilles
The sunlike, the killer. He is without mercy

As he is without the imagination that he is
Without mercy. There is nothing to the East of him
Except the camera, which is almost entirely without

Understanding of what it sees in him,
His hat, his gun, his gloves, his homely and
Heartbreaking canteen, empty on the ground.

*v*

The Anasazi drink from underground rivers.
The petroglyph cries out in the silence of the rock
The tourist looks at. The past is beautiful.

How few the implements and how carefully made
The dwelling place, against the wind and heat.
Looking at a photograph, as at a petroglyph,

How little there is to go on. "The darkest objects
Reflect almost no light, or none at all,
Causing no changes in the salt in the emulsion."

In the brilliant light and heart-stifling heat,
The scratchings on the surface of the rock,
Utterings, scriptions, bafflings of the spirit,

The bewildered eye reads nonsense in the dazzle;
In the black depth of the rock the river says nothing,
Reflectionless, swift, intent, purposeless, flowing.

*vi*

A picture of Eakins and a couple of other people,
One of them Murray, bathing in a river,
The Cohansey, near Fairton, New Jersey; Eakins

An old man, Murray not young; the other man,
Elderly, smiling, "probably Charlie Boyers."
They are patiently waiting for the picture to be taken.

It is a summer evening. The photograph
Is overexposed, so the light and the water are almost
Impossible to distinguish one from the other,

In their mutual weakness; an oarless rowboat waits
In the water, just clear of the rivergrass and weeds;
The opposite bank of the river is hard to see

In the washy blankness of the light; the sallow
Flat South Jersey landscape, treeless almost,
Almost featureless, stretches vaguely beyond.

# Graveyard

A writing I can't read myself: the picture
Of my father, taken a couple of years
Before he died; he is sitting alone some place
I don't know; maybe one of the meetings
He took to going to, trying to keep
His place in the world; he is smiling a little,
Cigarette smoke drifting away; he looks
Courteous, as always, not easy to know.

The side of a hill, nothing but a place;
Grass, dirt, a few scattered sticks, some stones,
The shadow of a tree; *Eurydice,*
*My father;* speaking the words as they are spoken
The meaning closes itself up; a manuscript
Written in a language only the dead speak.

# Counterpart

The last poem in this section of the book,
A counterpart to the one my great-grandfather
Wrote lines of, in his letter home: the ripening
Fruit, the purity of intention and deed
In the context of blood and error, the river
That has flowed in every man's ear from generation
To generation. When my great-grandfather preached,
One day, "a wonderful visitation of
The Holy Spirit came down upon the church.
It seemed to fall on men and women alike
Until upon all there was one baptism of the Holy
Fire, and he was thus in his little church
Consecrated to God in the work of preaching."
I found the letter in a metal box in my dead father's

Apartment; the place was shadowy even in the daytime;
Mild, early in September, quiet outside
On the street, and in the apartment; the television
Going, the sound turned off, images flickering
And fluttering inside the lighted screen,
Shaking and gesturing, beseeching the attention.
The ink of the faded ancient writing flowed
Across the page, flowed and lapsed, lapsed into
Forgetfulness; the morning air, the blankness

Of the light, a vapor, a shadow moving,
An unidentified man, selfhood altered.
"I am a child of the earth and of the sky.
But give me quickly the cold water to drink
That flows from Memory's source, from Lebadeia."

**VII**

# Rereading Old Writing

Looking back, the language scribbles.
What's hidden, having been said?
Almost everything? Thrilling to think
There was a secret there somewhere,
A bird singing in the heart's forest.

Two people sitting by a river;
Sunlight, shadow, some pretty trees;
Death dappling in the flowing water;
Beautiful to think about,
Romance inscrutable as music.

Out of the ground, in New Jersey, my mother's
Voice, toneless, wailing—beseeching?
Crying out nothing? A winter vapor,
Out of the urn, rising in the yellow
Air, an ashy smear on the page.

The quiet room floats on the waters,
Buoyed up gently on the daylight;
The branch I can see stirs a little;
Nothing to think about; writing
Is a way of being happy.

*What's going to be in this place?*
*A person entering a room?*
*Saying something? Signaling?*
*Writing a formula on a blackboard.*
*Something not to be understood.*

# DWELLING PLACES: POEMS AND TRANSLATIONS (1993)

*"Even unto this present hour we hunger, and thirst, and are naked, and are buffeted, and have no certain dwelling place."*

—1 Corinthians 4:11

I

# Strabo Reading Megasthenes

According to Megasthenes' own account
The wild man has no mouth with which to eat,

But only a breathing-orifice to breathe with.
He lives on the odor of fruits, and of flowers blooming,

Or on the smell of faraway roasting meat.

# *Dives*

The dogheaded wildman sleeps in the back alley,
Behind the fence with bittersweet adorned,
In the corner of the garden over near
Where the viburnum flowers or fails to flower,
Depending on whether or not we water it.
Many times over again it has survived.
The leaves are homely, crudely rough-cut, with
A texture like sandpaper; an unluscious green,
Virtuous in look, not really attractive;
Like Kent in *Lear* plainspoken, a truth-teller,
Impatient with comparison as with deceit.

The wildman sleeps in the maple-shaded alley
Hidden behind the garden fence behind
The wooden garden seat weathering gray
In the corner of the garden over near
Where the Orson Welles Movie Theater used to be,
From which in former days you faintly heard
The voices of the great dead stars still vying
In rich complaint, or else in exaltation
Of meeting or farewell, in rituals
Of wit o'ermastered, or in ecstasy
Of woe beyond the experience of saints.

In the alley between the yard and the old theater
The wildman is, covered with leaves or clad
In the bark of our indigenous flourishing trees,
Elaborately enscrolled and decorated
With the names of heavenly pity; there he sleeps
In the freedom of his distress among abandoned
Containers of paint, eggshell and offwhite tincts,
Umbers both raw and burnt, vermilion, rose,
Purples, and blues, and other hues and shades,
Close by the tangled roll of wire screening,
Under a scribbled hieroglyphic sign.

# The Guest Ellen at the Supper
# for Street People

The unclean spirits cry out in the body
Or mind of the guest Ellen in a loud voice
Torment me not, and in the fury of her unclean
Hands beating the air in some kind of unending torment—
Nobody witnessing could possibly know the event
That cast upon her the spell of this enchantment.

Almost all the guests are under some kind of enchantment:
Of being poor day after day in the same body;
Of being witness still to some obscene event;
Of listening all the time to somebody's voice
Whispering in the ear things divine or unclean,
In the quotidian of unending torment.

One has to keep thinking there was some source of torment,
Something that happened someplace else, unclean.
One has to keep talking in a reasonable voice
About things done, say, by a father's body
To or upon the body of Ellen, in enchantment
Helpless, still by the unforgotten event

Enchanted, still in the old forgotten event
A prisoner of love, filthy Ellen in her torment,
Guest Ellen in the dining hall in her body,

Hands beating the air in her enchantment,
Sitting alone, gabbling in her garbled voice
The narrative of the spirits of the unclean.

She is wholly the possessed one of the unclean.
Maybe the spirits came from the river. The enchantment
Entered her, maybe, in the Northeast Kingdom. The torment,
A thing of the waters, gratuitous event,
Came up out of the waters and entered her body
And lived in her in torment and cried out in her voice.

It speaks itself over and over again in her voice,
Cursing maybe or not a familiar obscene event
Or only the pure event of original enchantment
From the birth of the river waters, the pure unclean
Rising from the source of things, in a figure of torment
Seeking out Ellen, finding its home in her poor body.

Her body witness is, so also is her voice,
Of torment coming from unknown event;
Unclean is the nature and name of the enchantment.

# Committee

Coldly the sun shone down on the moonlit scene.
Our committee stirred uneasily in its sleep.
Better not know too much too soon all about it.
The knees of grammar and syntax touched each other,
Furtive in pleasure under the oaken table.

The river lay not moving under the light
Of the shadowy earthly winter lunar scene.
*The ends of justice are determined in*
*The conditions of our sleep.* The spellbound scene
Arranged itself in a traditional way,

Transfixed and perfectly still. Unspoken agreements
Spoke volumes on the bookshelves of the room.

# Civilization and Its Discontents

Under the burin's meditative gaze,
Caught in the cross-hatching and close-working
Of the great engraving of the great painting
*Fête Vénitienne,* entangled in
The entrapment of the scription, as if in vines
Entangled, or the entanglement of the veins,
It is Watteau himself, a naked soul,
Suffering the humiliation and pain
Of the company of fellow human beings,
Dressed up as a country shepherd pretending to play
The bagpipe or musette for them to dance to,
Looking over at what's-his-name, at Vleughels,
Monstrously civilized great Turkey cock
Here shown displaying all his gorgeous plumage
In grandiose dance, while all about in studied
Mutual disposition others were,
And Venus was, presiding over the scene,
And over all this the great embroidered trees.

# The Blind People

—*Baudelaire*

What is the difference between the unlimited
Blackness they walk in this ridiculous
Fashion through, and the eternal silence?
The sounds of the city, with all its laughter and music,
Are a denial I walk through with my stupid
Questions when I look at them. What are they
Looking up at the sky for, with such blind
Scrutinizing? Just think about them. How foolish,
And terrible, they look; weird; sleepwalkers;
Puppets on a string, the divine light gone
Forever from their eyes; and still they keep on
Staring up at the sky; they never bow
Their dreaming heads in noble meditation
Over the pavements of the raucous city.

# The Proselyte

A man the unclean spirits had gotten into
Got into the parish hall on Tuesday night.

The unclean spirits poured out through his skin
In the form of filth and cried out in that form,

And cried out in the form of how he went
Rapidly back and forth as if on many

Errands to one person and another
Or to nobody, up and down the parish hall,

Little trips back and forward rapidly,
Like a wasp or fly, hysterical with purpose,

Battering himself against our difference.
There was authority in him as he went

Carrying his message to one of us and another.
Who had condemned him to this filth and to

This unavailing rage? And the little voice
Crying out something in the body's cage?

The voice was pitifully small, as if
From someplace else or time of childhood, say,

Or country other, telling us something no one
In the parish hall could possibly understand,

Rabbinical, as if of ancient learning
Knowledgeable, and unintelligible,

A proselyte, the morphemes were uncouth.
His body was clad in the black of the unclean spirits.

And then he was gone away from the dining room,
A wasp trapped in a house, desperately trying,

Flying from one room into another room,
How to get out of the place in which it was,

Or else to carry the message to some place other.
He went to the phone on the wall of the hall outside

And said into the phone whatever it was he was saying,
And tore the phone out of the wall and talked to the wall,

Telling it things in the tiny faroff doleful
Insect crying voice in that other language.

And then he went to the outside door and said
To the outside door of the parish hall whatever

It was he said to us and the phone and the wall;
And then he was gone away into the night.

**II**

# A Young Woman

That she, with such gifts given,
In the abundance and grace

Of her youth and sweetness,
As if in a garden, walking,

In a summer of freshness
And of the wind lifting

And falling in a lavishing
Of light and penultimate

Shadow, that she should falter
At all through this phase,

Pressing, with hand outstretched,
The surface of the future,

As one who is blind presses
The surface of darkness,

Of corridor, or wall,
For any assurance at all,

May she be blessed
In this faltering forward.

# *Goodnight*

Lying in bed and waiting to find out
Whatever is going to happen: the window shade

Making its slightest sound as the night wind,
Outside, in the night, breathes quietly on it;

It is parental hovering over the infantile;
Something like that; it is like being a baby,

And over the sleep of the baby there is a father,
Or mother, breathing, hovering; the streetlight light

In the nighttime branches breathing quietly too;
Altering; realtering; it is the body breathing;

The crib of knowing: something about what the day
Will bring; and something about what the night will hold,

Safely, at least for the rest of the night, I pray.

# Nocturnal

It is always among sleepers we walk.
We walk in their dreams. None of us
Knows what he is as he walks
In the dream of another. *Tell me my name.*
Your tongue is blurred, honeyed with error.
Your sleep's truth murmurs its secret.

*Tell me your name.* Out at the edge,
Out in the cold, out in the cold
That came into the house in your clothes
The wind's hands hold onto nothing,
Moaning, over the edge of the cliff
The wind babble unintelligible.

# Abyss

—*Baudelaire*

Pascal's abyss was with him everywhere.
Everything is an abyss. Anything
That is done; that happens; is thought; is put into words.
I can't begin to tell you how many times
The fear in the sound of the wind has made my skin creep.

The deep; the long white empty beach stretching on
For ever; the silence; the desire of falling.
God has written out something on the face of the dark
In a hand absolutely sure of what it is doing.

I am afraid of sleep because I am afraid
Of a hole empty with horror. I can see nothing
Out of my window but infinity.
My acrophobic spirit is falling in love—
To be nowhere!—free of being, form, and name!

# Name

I wish I could recall now the lines written across the surface of my dream.
They said Name investigated the possibility of its own
happiness muttering and frowning preoccupied so that it noticed
nobody else at all though somehow you could tell that it knew somebody
was standing there in the doorway looking in at it and watching
what it was doing rummaging in desk drawers opening notebooks shutting
them up again writing down something or other on a scrap of paper
which would very soon be carelessly thrown away in a wastebasket and
go off in the trash somewhere out of the city burning stinking
       unrecoverable although not biodegradable.

# Of Rhyme

The task is the discovering of a rhyme
Whose consequence is just though unforeknown
Either in its completion having been
Prepared for though in secret all the time

Or in the way each step of the way brings in
To play with one another in the game
Considerations hitherto unknown,
New differences discovering the same.

The discovering is an ordering in time
Such that one seems to chance upon one's own
Birth name strangely engraved upon a stone
In consequence of the completion of the rhyme.

# *Epigram*

As with the skill of verses properly managed
The little river quietly makes its way
Along the valley and through the local village
Below the smiling hospitable house,
Easily flowing over the shining stones,
Trochee, and anapest, pyrrhic, and also spondee,
Under the heartbeat easy governance
Of long-continued metrical discipline.

Its fields and woods in their good order are
A figure for the manners of that house:
Disposed for intelligent pleasure, and for welcome.

# Autumn

*—Rilke*

The autumn leaves are falling,
Falling as if from far
Heavenly groves whose leaves
Are gesturing as they fall,
Hands protesting their falling.

The earth is falling too,
Falling through the night
Among indifferent stars.

See, this hand is falling.
All of us are falling.
It is in everything.

(Yet there is One who holds
Carefully in His hand
Everything falling forever.)

# Garden Dog

In the winter, out in the winter
Sunlight, watched from the upstairs

Window by the binocular eye,
Out in the winter light

The dog is wandering, sniffing
For enemies burrowed in Ireland

Sometime in the nineteenth century.
What's in a dog's heart?

The terrier brown coat
Touched into orange flame,

Blue, purple, pink,
By the binocular gaze,

The brilliant monster is wandering,
Smelling the winter air.

The wind is light. The light
Is wandering, blown by the breezes.

What's in the way the sun shines down?
Sniffing the sticks and stones,

Sniffing the dirt and dormant
Unflourishing grass in the garden,

Out in the winter light.

# Horses

*—for Tom Sleigh*

It is true that, as he said, the horses,
When the lightning signaled something
Along the horizon, acknowledged the signaling,

Moving about in extraordinary beauty
Of shifting and neighing, flicker of ear,
Changings of pace, slidings, turnings,

The delicate legs finding out something
The ground could tell them, interpreting
The sky's statement of oncoming darkness.

The storm was doing whatever it does,
Matrix of signaling, along the horizon.
In the valley the houses were brilliantly

Clear, the storm's darkness was making
Possible a perfect delineation,
The houses' edges brimming with light.

# Unos Caballos

—*Jorge Guillén*

There are several horses grazing in the field,
Motionless almost, untroubled as the grass

Silently growing there in the light of the natural
Morning before the beginning of anything human.

Docile in the confines of the pasture,
These hairy, unyoked, idle, quiet creatures,

In vegetative peacefulness show no sign
Of understanding. Their tranquil eyes and ears

Know nothing of the vigil that they keep.
The serenity of heaven is realized

In their obliviousness of it, grazing there.

# Roof

Four or five men on the high roof
Of the apartment house I see from out my window,

Angels or other beings from an element
Other than ours but similar although

Superior so bright and clear, perfected
In diminutive particular; angels

Or little brilliant demons or simian
Creatures with nose-and-mouth mask snouts

Against the fumes of the material
A tiny glittering machine is putting down.

The fumes are visible and drift away,
Like martyred souls made visible in the radiant air.

# A Morning Song

A bird cried out among the first things of the morning.
I dreamed about murders all night long.

The stone changed color among the shadows as the sun came up.
It was the bird's cry that startled up the stone.

# Of Violets

—Politian

O beautiful violets, seeming to give such promise
Of the fulfillment of love, the gift of her
Whom I love, what is the nectar the tender winds
Have scattered over your petals, making them fragrant?
What is the place of your birth? Was it under the care
Of radiant Venus, there in the fields near the spring
Of Acidalia? Was it under the care
Of the god of love in the Idalian grove?

It must be that these are the same flowers
With which the Muses decorate their lyres
To play upon on the flowerbank of Permessus,
That these are the same flowers with which the maidens
Hora, Gratia, Aurora, have adorned themselves
In the hour of the opening day. These must be the same
Flowers that bloom in the violetbeds of the garden
Of the Hesperides, in the silent grove
The held breath of the wind possesses. These
Violets are the springtime offering of Chloris;

The virtuous shades of the dead come back to play
Among the grasses the violets intersperse.

Too happy violets, which that hand plucked
That wrenched me, miserable, from myself—
She held you, violets, to her lips, perhaps;
Perhaps her lips and breath have breathed on you
The breath of her whom I love, the changing colors
Of her breathing, making you blush and pale;
From the breath of her lips your fragrance is breathed upon you;
The sovereignty of her fragrance clings to you.

O most fortunate violets, who are
My life and my delight, the place of keeping,
The haven of my heart's longing, violets,
Whom I touch and kiss in pain in thought of her,
These tears I shed nourish the fires of love
Whose slow burning issues in these tears.
Be with me now forever, violets;
Let neither the heat of summer nor winter's cold
Deprive me of your solace, solace of pain;
Stay with me now, perpetual in beauty,
O violets, O quietness of heart,
For I am in the wretchedness of love,

Creature of sighs and weeping, because of my lady.

# Levis Exsurgit Zephirus

*—Goliardic*

The wind stirs lightly as the sun's
Warmth stirs in the new season's
Moment when the earth shows everything
She has, her fragrance on everything.

The spring royally in his excitement
Scatters the new season's commandment
Everywhere, and the new leaves open,
The buds open, and begin to happen.

The winged and the fourfooted creatures
According to their several natures
Find or build their nesting places;
Each unknowingly rejoices.

Held apart from the season's pleasure
According to my separate nature
Nevertheless I bless and praise
The new beginning of the new days,

Seeing it all, hearing it all,
The leaf opening, the first bird call.

# Herbsttag

*—Rilke*

Now is the right time, Lord. Summer is over.
Let the autumn shadows drift upon the sundials,
And let the wind stray loose over the fields.

Summer was abundant. May the last fruits be full
Of its promise. Give them a last few summer days.
Bring everything into its completion, Lord,
The last sweetness final in the heavy wine.

Who has no house will never have one now;
Who is alone will spend his days alone;
Will wake to read some pages of a book;
Will write long letters; wander unpeacefully
In the late streets, while the leaves stray down.

# The Lesson

*—from the Latin of Samuel Johnson*

The stream still flows through the meadow grass,
As clear as it was when I used to go in swimming,
Not good at it at all, while my father's voice
Gently called out through the light of the shadowy glade,
Trying to help me learn. The branches hung down low
Over those waters made secret by their shadows.
My arms flailed in a childlike helpless way.

And now the sharp blade of the axe of time
Has utterly cut away that tangle of shadows.
The naked waters are open to the sky now
And the stream still flows through the meadow grass.

# In the Garden

The impatiens in the tub, beside the wooden bench
I'm sitting on, has leaves that are uniformly
A light green almost to the state of water,
Different from the impatiens twenty feet away,
Over by the birdbath. Are they a different
Species or are the differences the result
Of different conditions of light or earth?
The green of these leaves is almost an absence of green,
And the stalks look like rays of light under water.
The blossoms are pure white, with yellow centers.

I just this minute noticed that there are yellow
Five-petalled flowers blooming in the little
Patch of clover in the ground beside the tub.
These yellow flowers have centers of a pale-
Yellow growing out of a tender matrix
Of green; and growing out of the same stalk
Is a pod shaped like a little zucchini, or steeple,
Pointed, tall by comparison with the flowers.

There is something springlike and free about the littleness,
Oddness, and lightness of this combination of things,
Observed here at the very tag end of summer,
In my good fortune.

Another little plant,
A weed I also don't know the name of,
With a white flower shaped like a deep cup
And with blue-tipped sexual parts, lies in the grass,
The fallen maiden of some casual violence.
The whole plucked stalk is an event in time:
A number of blossoms one above the other,
But some blossoms more fully out than others,
In an intricately regular scale or series.
Of course, since the flower is plucked, it isn't really
An event in time, but only the record of an event.

Now there are a few leaves falling from the ash tree
In the steady mild wind. What's to come of all this
Ill-informed staring at little flowers and
Enigmatic misleading stalks and leaves?
It isn't autumn yet. There will be late autumn flowers.

When the wind started up suddenly just now,
When I was sitting in the garden reading Edward Thomas,
When I was looking at the back wall of our house,
Soon to be different after the new porch is built,
When I had just had lunch with a friend who spoke
Of how she used to be a lush and now
Eats no meat, no sugar, and no dairy,
When my daughter in another part of the garden
Was reading *The Mayor of Casterbridge,* and the branches
Of the white fringe and the witch hazel shifted
Suddenly, horizontally, and other branches
In the garden suddenly stirred and shifted, it was
As if these trees and bushes, the white ash, the sugar-
Maple, the deutzia, the young unflowering pear tree,

Had all suddenly had the same idea,
Of motion and quiet sound and the changing light,
A subtle, brilliant, and a shadowy idea.

# Roman Elegy VIII

—*Goethe*

When you tell me that you were unpopular as a child,
And that your mother spoke of you in a rueful

Tone of voice, and that all this seemed to go on
For a very long time, the slow time that it took

For you to grow up, I believe you, and I enjoy
Thinking about that odd, awkward child.

The grapevine-flower, you know, is nothing much,
But the ripened fruit gives pleasure to men and gods.

# When We Were Children

—'der Wilde Alexander' (fl. late 13th C.)

I remember how, at that time, in this meadow,
We used to run up and down, playing our games,
Tag and games of that sort; and looked for wildflowers,
Violets and such. A long time ago.
Now there are only these cows, bothered by flies,
Only these cows, wandering about in the meadow.

I remember us sitting down in the field of flowers,
Surrounded by flowers, and playing she loves me not,
She loves me; plucking the flower petals.
My memory of childhood is full of those flowers,
Bright with the colors of garlands we wore in our dancing
And playing. So time went by among the wildflowers.

Look over there near those trees at the edge of the woods.
Right over there is where we used to find
Blueberry bushes, blackberry bushes, wild strawberries.
We had to climb over rocks and old walls to get them.
One day a man called out to us: "Children, go home."
He had been watching from somewhere in the woods.

We used to feast on the berries we found in that place
Till our hands and mouths were stained with the colors of all
The berries, the blackberries, strawberries, and the blueberries.
It was all fun to us, in the days of our childhood.
One day a man called out, in a doleful voice:
"Go home, children, go home, there are snakes in that place."

One day one of the children went into the grass
That grows high near the woods, among the bushes.
We heard him scream and cry out. He came back weeping.
"Our little horse is lying down and bleeding.
Our pony is lying down. Our pony is dying.
I saw a snake go crawling off in the grass."

Children, go home, before it gets too dark.
If you don't go home before the light has gone,
If you don't get home before the night has come,
Listen to me, you will be lost in the dark,
Listen to me, your joy will turn into sorrow.
Children, go home, before it gets to be dark.

*There were five virgins lingered in a field.*
*The king went in with his bride and shut the doors.*
*The palace doors were shut against the virgins.*
*The virgins wept, left standing in the field.*
*The servants came and stripped the virgins naked.*
*The virgins wept, stripped naked, in the field.*

**III**

# Mnemosyne

—*Hölderlin*

*i*

Flowers, streams, hills, meadows, valleys—
Everything beautiful praises the Lord,
In order to find out whether or not He is.

A wedding day is beautiful. Human arrangements,
The keeping of laws to shelter in, can break your heart.
He can change any or all of it just as He pleases.
Law is nothing He needs of what we know of it.

The hero desires to be in that condition,
Where Truth *is* Being. The hero goes to the edge
And looks down over into whatever is there, or not,
In terror. God cannot do everything.
He cannot, like the hero, be in terror.

But everything is as it is, one way or another.
What does it all add up to, after all? Praise Him.

Peaceful scene: the sunlight on the lawns;
The shadowy branches over the dry paths;
The smoke blossoming from the chimney tops;
The lark song almost lost in the perfect sky;
The sheep and cattle feeding in the fields,
Well-tended; the snow in the high meadows, flowering.

Value shining and flourishing everywhere.

Two people went this way, passing the cross
Once placed there long ago for the pious dead,
Two wanderers, one of them raging.

*iii*

Under the figtree my Achilles lies,
Who died for me; and Ajax, near Scamander,
Under the sound of the wind, at the grotto's mouth,
In a foreign country, far from Salamis.

Heroes have died, in one way or another.

Some were astonished in the bloodsoaked field,
In the experience of their fate, surrounded;
Patroclus in the armor of the king;
Others, in torment and bewilderment,
By their own hand, compelled by heaven.

Things go all wrong when He takes hold of one of us.
But everything is as it is, one way or another.

**IV**

# Harvesters Resting

—*after Millet*

In the middle of the day, in the great shadow
Of the grain stack, the harvesters
Are resting and having their midday meal.

Boaz is approaching with a woman.
Meticulous as cattle in their attention
To the task of resting and feeding,
Some of them seem not to have noticed.

Others regard her with the slow,
Blind, thorough look that cattle have,
Spellbound in the noontime heat.

# Mary in Old Age

> Yet, though dread Powers, that work in mystery, spin
> Entanglings of the brain; though shadows stretch
> O'er the chilled heart—reflect, far, far within,
> Hers is a holy Being, freed from Sin,
> She is not what she seems, a forlorn Wretch,
> But delegated Spirits comforts fetch
> For her from heights that reason may not win.
> —Wordsworth, *Miscellaneous Sonnets,* III, 36

I

*Mary's House*

The bruised eyes and diffused radiant
Face, anger *and* joy fused
In a question,
By what possible measure contained?

A skull's blood beating entirely
Uninstructed against

Whatever the world withheld against
The answer.

Nobody knew the answer.
The trees' dark bodies pressed up
Against the house, like night by day,
How like a night by night.

## Mary's Room at the Nursing Home

The room was like a room in a rented house
By the sea in the summer. The sun shone in

Flatly and plainly, and sunlight and shadow
Were disposed forthrightly and reasonably

Across the surface of things, for instance on
The brown linoleum floor or on the simple

Pine table painted a chalky green. There were decal
Flowers on the headboard and footboard of the bed,

Ignorant and cheerful about where they were.
As in a room to which one goes on vacation,

A rented place by the sea, there were very few
Things one could call one's own, and these had a vivid

Prominence: an open book on a table,
A vase of blue and white cornflowers, a brass clock.

Can Mary have been reading? Is the madness a hoax?
But the book on the table was a Harlequin romance

The attendant must just that moment have left off reading.
It was hot as anything. The curtains mimed

The letting in of air. Strangely girlish and wasted,
Mary lay on the little single bed

In a flowered summer dress, a naked Maja,
Or like Olympia in the painting by Manet,

Careless of everything, wanton, royal.

### The Tower of Babel

She babbled barbarously and bravely,
With bravado and bravura,
A baby in a babushka, with a balalaika.

She was "a gate of God," a Babeler,
"Though babbling only to the Vale
Of sunshine and of flowers,

Bringing unto me
a tale of visionary hours."

## IV

## *Of Others Who Were There*

There was: the old lady in the nursing home
Who kept coming up to me and standing much too close
To me, sniffing at my body or my soul
As if it was something deliciously stinking,

Thrilling to her, or else a flowering bush,
Nourishment for a ravenous questioning;
Staring into my ear the way the child
In the comic routine long ago in the movies

Stared silently into the coils of the ear
Of the man sitting there next to the child,
Trying to watch the movie on the screen,
Driven wild inside by the child's relentless gaze:

As if the ear could speak its secrets back.

*Mary Interpreter*

Not a babble exactly, but words carefully chosen
To question the nature of her experience

In the bafflement of its own imprisoning nonsense.
Of the flowers I brought her on that summer day:

"When are you going to take them home and use them?"
And, "Yes, they were here, but I didn't see them,"

And, looking once again at the bouquet,
More closely, earnestly, and with suspicion:

"What is that? *Why did it go wrong?*"
Rocking a little in the rocking chair, she said,

"*I don't want to stay here. I want to stop it.*"
Was "here" the nursing home? Was it the chair?

The condition she was in? Her life? Life? The body?
Which of these things was it she wanted to stop?

Was she imprisoned in a world whose meanings
She was so familiar with that she needed to make

No translations at all, and no translation would be
Anything but fatuous? Thus "Life" seems melodramatic,

Too large and general to fit the case.
But "the chair" seems too small. And "the nursing home"

Too obviously the right answer to be so.
In my reason and health I was outside this world,

Translating her words with a too easy confidence.
But Mary was there, imprisoned in it, sovereign.

The scene changed in the way I experienced it.
It was as if I wasn't in the room

But in the empty lobby of some building.
Mary was in an open elevator,

Old-fashioned, ornate, and beautiful.
The elevator kept moving up and down,

Kept going down to the hell below—when I
Leaned over and looked down then I could see

The suffering and also I could hear
Sounds of the suffering too—then up again

To the hellish heaven above—peering up there
Through the elevator shaft I saw and heard

The transcendental hilarious suffering there.
I heard voices as if there was singing or quarreling.

The Otis elevator never stopped at all.
Mary's body and spirit kept passing back and forth

Before my eyes, vivid, free of the conditions
In terms of which her sympathetic friend,

Standing in the deserted hallway, saw her
Carried up and down in the elevator.

Over and over I saw her going past,
Clinging to the bars, gesticulating,

Frantic, confusingly like a figure of joy.
In the heat of the room on the summer day

Mary, standing now, began to unzip her dress,
With a slowness and persistence that suggested

An indecent purpose, a naked revelation
Of body or soul, embarrassing to a visitor

There at the nursing home on a kind errand.
Perhaps she only wanted to unzip the dress

A little way, because of the summer heat.
But something about it seemed to refuse the suggestion.

There was a concentration and seriousness,
Oblivious of the visitor and his thoughts,

As when she looked so earnestly at the bouquet.
We were in the same room and not in the same room.

I was in the same room. She was in a shirt of fire.
She was out on a plain crossed by steppewinds.

*Matthew 12: 43–45*

When the unclean spirit goes out of a person,
She walks for days and nights through the dry places,
Looking for rest, and never finding any.
And then she says, "I will go home to my house,

From which I came." And so Mary goes there.
She finds it nicely swept and cleanly kept,
And pleasantly furnished, and garnished with flowers,
And empty, as if waiting for her to come home.

And then the unclean spirit goes and finds the other
Unclean spirits. They come to her house together,
And get into the house, and live there, and it is worse
For her, much worse, than it had earlier been.

# *Prayer to the Gods of the Night*

*—Babylonian*

The gates of the town are closed. The princes
Have gone to sleep. The chatter of voices

Has quieted down. Doorbolts are fastened.
Not until morning will they be opened.

The gods of the place, and the goddess,
Ishtar, Sin, Adad, and Shamash,

Have gone into the quiet of the sky,
Making no judgments. Only

The voice of a lone wayfarer
Calls out the name of Shamash or Ishtar.

Now house and field are entirely silent.
The night is veiled. A sleepless client

In the still night waits for the morning.
Great Shamash has gone into the sleeping

Heaven; the father of the poor,
The judge, has gone into his chamber.

May the gods of the night come forth—the Hunter,
The Bow, the Wagon, the Yoke, the Viper,

Irra the valiant, the Goat, the Bison,
Girra the shining, the Seven, the Dragon—

May the stars come forth in the high heaven.

*Establish the truth in the ritual omen;*
*In the offered lamb establish the truth.*

# Envoi

Let these not be the black, imaginary

Flowers of hell, nihilotropic,

Turning their iron faces toward

No light but the light of the dead letter.

*from* GILGAMESH: A NEW RENDERING
IN ENGLISH VERSE (1992)

# *Tablet VII*

I

Enkidu dreamed that the gods had met in council:
Anu said: "They have killed the Bull of Heaven

and killed Huwawa. One of them must die,
the one of them who felled the tallest cedar."

Then Enlil said that Enkidu must die
but Gilgamesh, the gifted, must not die.

And Shamash said: "The two of them went together,
companions on my errand into the Forest.

Why then should Enkidu, who went, companion,
into the Cedar Forest on my errand,

why should he die?" Angry Enlil said:
"You went with them as if *you* were companion,

day after day as they went upon their journey
to violate the Forest and kill the guardian."

## II

And so it was that Enkidu fell sick.
Gilgamesh looked at him and weeping said:

"Why am I left to live while my brother dies?
Why should he die and I be spared to live?"

Enkidu said: "Must I now go to sit
among the dead, in the company of the dead

without my brother?" Gilgamesh said: "Must I
now sit outside the door of the house of the dead

while Enkidu sits in the house of the dead among
the shadow companions?" Then Enkidu cursed the portal

made of the cedar tree they had felled in the Forest:
"You stupid wooden door that does not hear.

I searched for twenty leagues to find the cedar,
tallest of all, with which to make a great

monument for the city, suitable
to celebrate the story of the famous

victory in the Forest over the guardian.
If I had known that this would happen to me

I would have taken my ax and chopped to bits
the wood of the cedar I helped bring to the city.

Grant that some future king destroy the portal
or that a god obliterate from it

utterly the name of Enkidu.
May the name of the companion be forgotten."

Gilgamesh listened to him and weeping said:
"The stormy heart of Enkidu the companion

rages with understanding of the fate
the high gods have established for mankind.

To rage against the gods of heaven is futile.
What Enlil has ordained cannot be changed.

This is the truth told in the frightening dream.
Gilgamesh the brother will pray to the gods,

beseeching the high gods to spare the companion;
Gilgamesh the king will build a statue

to celebrate the fame of Enkidu."


III


In the early hours of the next morning dawning,
Enkidu, sleepless, weeping, cried out to Shamash:

"As for the hunter who saw me in the grasslands,
may the creatures which he hunts, the gazelles and the others,

get away from him free. May the hunter starve
because he saw me at the watering place.

Fill in his hunting pits, unset his traps,
so that he can no longer be a hunter."

With the first light of the early morning dawning,
Enkidu, sleepless, cried out against the harlot:

"As for the harlot who brought me to the city,
this is the curse of Enkidu against her:

May the garbage of the city be what you eat.
May you drink what flows along the alley gutters.

May you importune in the alley shadows.
May you have no home. May you sleep on the city doorsteps.

May there be signs of vomit on your clothes.
May all men curse and revile you and turn away.

Because of you the creatures fled from me,
who dwelt with them and ranged the hills with them."

Then Shamash spoke and said to Enkidu:
"Why do you curse the temple prostitute?

Because of her you eat the food and drink
the palace affords. Because of her you wear

the garments suitable for a prince to wear;
you sit in the place of honor nearest the king;

the great ones of the earth bow down before you.
Gilgamesh is your friend and your companion.

The grief of Gilgamesh for you will be
the cause of woe and wailing in the city.

Gilgamesh the king will build a statue
to celebrate the fame of Enkidu.

When you are gone, then Gilgamesh will wear
the skins of beasts and hairy-bodied wander

grieving in the wilderness for you."
Enkidu heard what Shamash said to him,

and for a time his stormy heart was quiet.
He repented the curse and blessed the harlot, saying:

"This is the blessing of Enkidu on Shamhat:
May no man revile or curse or turn away.

May the old man comb his locks and beard to please you.
May the young unbuckle his belt in joy for you.

May your house be full of gifts, crystal and gold,
carnelian and lapis lazuli,

earrings and filigree ornaments, fine new clothes.
May the priests invite you with honor into the temple."

## IV

In the early hours of the next morning dawning,
Enkidu lay in his bed, fear in his belly.

He told a dream to Gilgamesh who was there.
"I had a dream. There was a noise in the sky

and a noise in the earth in answer. On a dark plain
I was alone. But there was one, a man,

with a lion head, and the paws of a lion too,
but the nails were talons, the talons of an eagle.

The face was dark. He took hold of me and seized me.
I fought with him, I hit at him, but he

kept moving about in the dark, too quick for me,
and then with a blow he capsized me like a raft.

I cried out in the dark to Gilgamesh,
'Two people, companions,' but the man overpowered me,

and raged like a wild bull over me in glory,
and Gilgamesh was afraid and did not help me.

Then I was changed into something like a bird,
with a bird's arms, as spindly as a bird's,

and feathered like a bird. He seized an arm
and led me to the dwelling of Irkalla,

the House of Darkness, the House of No Return.
No one comes back who ever enters there.

The garments that they wear are made of feathers.
The food they eat is clay, the drink is dirt.

Stillness and dust are on the door and door bolt.
There is no light of any sort at all.

Dead kings were there, and princes of old kingdoms,
dead high priests and acolytes were there,

dead chanters and anointers, bearers of ointments;
Etana was there and Sumuqan was there,

and on her throne Ereshkigal the Queen
of the Underworld, and kneeling before her was

Belit-Seri the Scribe who holds the tablet
on which the fate of everyone is written.

She turned her head and looked at us and said:
'Who has led here this latest to arrive?'"


v

Gilgamesh said: "The dream is terrible."
Enkidu said: "We went together through

the dangers of the Forest and we killed
the Bull of Heaven. Do not forget how we,

two people together, prevailed against the terror."
Enkidu lay suffering on the bed of terror

another day and another day and another,
and the long nights between, and day after day

the suffering of Enkidu grew worse.
On the twelfth day he raised up in his bed

and spoke these words to Gilgamesh and said:
"Gilgamesh, who encouraged me in the battle,

saying, 'Two people, companions, they can prevail,'
Gilgamesh is afraid and does not help me!"

After that Gilgamesh heard the death rattle.

# Tablet VIII

I

With the first light of the early morning dawning,
in the presence of the old men of the city,

Gilgamesh, weeping, mourned for Enkidu:
"It is Enkidu, the companion, whom I weep for,

weeping for him as if I were a woman.
He was the festal garment of the feast.

On the dangerous errand, in the confusions of noises,
he was the shield that went before in the battle;

he was the weapon at hand to attack and defend.
A demon has come and taken away the companion.

He ranged the hills together with the creatures
whose hearts delight to visit the watering places.

A demon has come and taken him away.
He was the first to find the way through the passes

to go to the Cedar Forest to kill Huwawa.
He sought the wilderness places to find the water

with which to quench our thirst on the way to the Forest.
Together we killed Huwawa; together we fought

the bellowing Bull of Heaven, and killed the Bull,
and together the two of us sat down to rest.

Then a demon came and took away the companion.
You are asleep. What has taken you into your sleep?

Your face is dark. How was your face made dark?"
Enkidu's eyes were unmoving in their sockets.

Gilgamesh touched the heart of the companion.
There was nothing at all. Gilgamesh covered

Enkidu's face with a veil like the veil of a bride.
He hovered like an eagle over the body,

or as a lioness does over her brood.


11

With the first light of the early morning dawning,
Gilgamesh said to Enkidu the companion:

"May the wild ass in the mountains braying mourn.
May the furtive panthers mourn for Enkidu,

the gazelles and the other grazing creatures mourn
for Enkidu at the wilderness watering places.

May the pathways to the Cedar Forest mourn.
May the passes through the mountains mourn for you.

May the old men of the city mourn, and those
who warned and blessed us on our journey mourn.

May the grasslands wail as if they were your mother.
May the gazelle your mother and the wild ass

your father mourn for Enkidu their child.
The milk you were suckled on was the milk of the creatures,

and the creatures taught you to graze in the wild pastures.
May the holy river mourn, the river Ulaja;

Euphrates mourn whose pure river waters
we made libations of, and drank the waters.

May the young men of the city who fought the Bull,
may they mourn for Enkidu who protected them.

May the farmer who sings of you as he works in the field
mourn as he works in the field, may the shepherds mourn,

who brought you the beer and the cooked food in their camp,
may they mourn for you because you protected them

so that they slept at night in peaceful sleep.
May the harlot weep for you who showed you her body

and showed you the things a woman knows how to do.
May the priests mourn in the rite of lamentation.

Listen to me, you elders of the city,
it is Enkidu, the companion, whom I weep for."


III

Gilgamesh called together the makers of statues,
lapidaries, forgers, workers in copper and gold,

and commanded that there be made a statue of him,
of Enkidu the companion, to honor his deeds.

And Gilgamesh spoke to Enkidu's memory, saying:
"You wore the garments suitable for a prince.

You sat in the place of honor nearest the king.
The great ones of the earth bowed down before you.

Gilgamesh was your friend and your companion.
Gilgamesh the king has built a statue

to celebrate the fame of Enkidu.
The grief of Gilgamesh for you has been

the cause of woe and wailing in the city.
Now you are gone, and Gilgamesh will wear

the skins of beasts and wander hairy-bodied
grieving in the wilderness for you."

With the first light of the early morning dawning,
he made an altar and on the altar offered,

in a carnelian bowl, an offering
of honey, and in another bowl, of lapis

lazuli made, an offering of butter:
these offerings to propitiate the god.

*from* THE ODES OF HORACE:
A TRANSLATION (1997)

# *Ode i.11*

*To Leuconoë*

Don't be too eager to ask
        What the gods have in mind for us,
What will become of you,
        What will become of me,
What you can read in the cards,
        Or spell out on the Ouija board.
It's better not to know.
        Either Jupiter says
This coming winter is not
        After all going to be
The last winter you have,
        Or else Jupiter says
This winter that's coming soon,
        Eating away the cliffs
Along the Tyrrhenian Sea,
        Is going to be the final
Winter of all. Be mindful.
        Take good care of your household.
The time we have is short.
        Cut short your hopes for longer.
Now as I say these words,
        Time has already fled

Backwards away—
        Leuconoë—
                Hold on to the day.

# *Ode i.18*

*To Varus*

For planting in the rich Tiburtine soil
Upon the slopes of Mt. Catillus, Varus,
Favor no plant before the sacred vine.
Bacchus commands that everything be hard
For him who abstains from wine, and Bacchus says
The troubles that wear away our days are not
Made easier by any other means.
After a drink or two who is it who
Complains about the hardships of his lot—
His poverty, or his service in the army?
Who fails to praise you then, O father Bacchus?
Who fails to praise you too, O queen of love?
And yet there is a lesson in the example
Of the fight between the Centaurs and the Lapiths,
That went so far too far at the drunken banquet.
And there's another in the Sithonian drinkers
Who think they tell right from wrong by squinting along
The disappearing line libidinous desire
Draws on the wet bartop. I would not dare
To stir you up, O Bacchus, against your will,
Nor will I be the one to betray to the light
The secret signs that you have covered over

In grape and ivy leaves. Bacchus, repress
The cymbal and the Berecynthian horn
And those who revel in that raucous music:
Blind love that has no eyes but for itself;
Vain Glory with its vacant head held high;
And barfly Faithlessness whose promiscuous tongue
Spills all its secrets into promiscuous ears.

# Ode i.14

*To the Republic*

O ship, O battered ship, the backward running waves

Are taking you out to sea again! O what to do?

O don't you see? O make for port! The wind's gone wild!

Your sails are torn! Your mast is shaking! Your oars are gone!

Your onboard gods gone overboard! How long, how long

Can the eggshell hull so frail hold out? O ship so proud,

Your famous name, your gilded stern, your polished decks,

Your polished brass, so useless now, O storm's play thing,

O ship my care, beware, beware the Cyclades!

# Ode i.37

*Of Cleopatra*

At last the day has come for celebration,
For dancing and for drinking, bringing out
The couches with their images of gods
Adorned in preparation for the feast.

Before today it would have been wrong to call
For the festive Caecuban wine from the vintage bins,
It would have been wrong while that besotted queen,
With her vile gang of sick polluted creatures,

Crazed with hope and drunk with her past successes,
Was planning the death and destruction of the empire.
But, comrades, she came to and sobered up
When not one ship, almost, of all her fleet

Escaped unburned, and Caesar saw to it
That she was restored from madness to a state
Of realistic terror. The way a hawk
Chases a frightened dove or as a hunter

Chases a hare across the snowy steppes,
His galleys chased this fleeing queen, intending

To put the monster prodigy into chains
And bring her back to Rome. But she desired

A nobler fate than that; she did not seek
To hide her remnant fleet in a secret harbor;
Nor did she, like a woman, quail with fear
At the thought of what it is the dagger does.

She grew more fierce as she beheld her death.
Bravely, as if unmoved, she looked upon
The ruins of her palace; bravely reached out,
And touched the poison snakes, and picked them up,

And handled them, and held them to her so
Her heart might drink its fill of their black venom.
In truth—no abject woman she—she scorned
In triumph to be brought in galleys unqueened

Across the seas to Rome to be a show.

# *Ode i.34*

*Of the God's Power*

Sparing and but perfunctory in my devotions,
Going my own way, wandering in my learnèd
Well-considered folly, now I must turn about,

And change my course, and sail for home and safety.
Jupiter, whose thunder and whose lightning
Require the clouds, just now, this minute, drove

His thundering chariot and his thundering horses
Right straight across a perfectly cloudless sky,
Unsettling streams and shaking the heavy ground

All the way down to the river Styx and out
To the end of the earth beyond Taenarus' seat,
Where Atlas holds up the sky upon his shoulders.

Oh yes, the god has power. Oh yes, he can
Raise up the low and bring the high things down.
Fortune's wings rustle as the choice is made.

# *Ode i.17*

Sometimes Faunus comes from Arcady
To fair Lucretilis, and while he's here
Sees to it that my goats are sheltered from
The summer heat and from the wind and rain.

Tyndaris, when this place falls under the spell
Of the rocks and hills of Ustica echoing
The sound of Faunus playing upon his pipe,
The wives of the rank male goat then feeling easy

Can wander through the woods in safety searching
For thyme and for arbutus where they hide,
Nor do the kids have anything to fear
From snakes nor from Mars' favorite, the wolf.

The gods protect me here because they know
That I and my Muse are ever devout and faithful.
And here, for you, from the horn of plenty flow
All the good things of our local fields and vines.

Here you can shade yourself from the heat of summer,
Singing a song about Penelope

And Circe of the glassy sea, and how
Both of them loved the wandering Ulysses.

Here you will sit, under these guardian plane trees,
Tasting the mild innocent wine of Lesbos;
Here Mars and Bacchus, Semele's child, will never
Contend to make trouble; and, untroubled here,

Protected, here in the garden, under these trees,
You will have nothing to fear from jealous Cyrus,
Tearing your dress, or disarranging your hair,
Pawing you with his cruel offending hands.

# Ode i.32

*To His Lyre*

Pray for a new song. You and I together
Under the trees in the shade, have played such songs
As could live beyond the end of the year, and longer,
    O lyre, O tortoise shell,

First stringed and tuned to make the beautiful music
Alcaeus played in the Grecian battle camp,
And, having survived the storm and brought his boat
    Safe to the wave-drenched beach,

Played on the beach his songs of Bacchus and
Of Venus and the child who clings to her,
And dark-haired dark-eyed Lycus whom he loved.
    Let us play a Roman song.

*O instrument of Phoebus Apollo's favor,*
*O gladly heard at Jupiter's table itself,*
*O medicine of sorrows, now bring forth*
    *The music I invoke.*

# Ode i. 24

How should this grief be properly put into words?
Melpomene, to whom the Father gave
The voice that to the music of the lyre
Flows out in mournful measure, teach me the art.

Can it be true that Quintilius lies in the sleep
That goes on without ever ending? Where then will Justice,
And Faith, the sister of Justice, and Decency,
And Truth that needs no ornament, find his equal?

Virgil, many are they who mourn for him,
But none like you who mourn so, ceaselessly.
Your pious grief, alas, can never persuade
The gods to alter the terms that gave him life.

Suppose that you were able to play the lyre
Even more skillfully than Orpheus played it,
Causing the very trees to listen to him,
What good would it do? Could the music restore

Blood to the veins of the empty shade of one
Who has died? How could the music persuade the god

To open the door he has shut, and shut once and for all,
The god whose horrid wand shepherds the dead

To where they are going down there to be shut away?
It is hard. But all of this must be endured,
And by endurance what can never be changed
Will be at last made easier in the heart.

*from* THE ECLOGUES OF VIRGIL:
A TRANSLATION (1999)

# Eclogue Five

*Menalcas*    *Mopsus*

*Menalcas*

    Mopsus, let us sit down together here
    In this elm and hazel grove, two good musicians,
    You at the shepherd's pipe and I at singing.

*Mopsus*

    You are the elder of us two, Menalcas,
    Therefore you should choose where we should be,
    Whether beneath these trees, within the shadows
    That change and move as the breezes move and change them,
    Or else within this cave that's near at hand—
    See how the vine has spread its tendrils round
    The entrance to the cave, with clustering flowers.

*Menalcas*

    You have no mountain rival but Amyntas.

*Mopsus*

    Do you think he wants to rival Apollo too?

*Menalcas*

    If you have one ready, Mopsus, play a song
    In praise of Phyllis your love, or in praise of Alcon,
    Or maybe play in fun one praising Codrus.
    Tityrus will watch the grazing flock.

*Mopsus*

        I think, instead, I'll try these verses I carved
        On a green beech tree the other afternoon.
        First I marked out the words and then marked out
        The music that I wrote to go with the words.
        See if Amyntas can do as well as this.

*Menalcas*

        It seems to me Amyntas yields to you
        As the willow bows to the pale green olive tree
        And the low wild nard gives precedence to the rose,

        But now we are in the cavern. Begin your song.

*Mopsus*

        "The hazels and the rivers testify
        How the Nymphs shed tears for Daphnis, as his mother,
        Embracing the wretched body of her child,
        So cruelly dead, cried out against the gods
        And against the stars. In the days of this event
        Nobody drove his cattle down to the brooks
        To drink the cooling water; no beast would drink;
        And, Daphnis, the woods, the wilderness mountains told us
        How, far away in Africa, the lions
        Mourning in the desert could be heard.
        It was Daphnis who yoked together the tigers to draw
        The chariot of Bacchus, and it was Daphnis

Who led the Bacchic dance, and Daphnis who bound
The vine-leaves and the fennel stalk together
To make the thyrsus of Bacchus. Just as the vine
Is the glory of the tree-trunk that it clings to,
Just as the grape is the glory of its vine,
Just as the bull is the glory of its herd,
And the flourishing corn of the soil it grows from, Daphnis,
You are the glory of all the rest of us.
Now that the Fates have taken you away,
Apollo has left our fields, and Pales too.
In the furrows where we hopefully planted barley,
Darnel and tares and sterile oat-grass grow;
Where the violet and purple narcissus were,
Now thistle flourishes and spiky thorn.
Scatter the ground with flowers, all you shepherds,
And shade with mourning trees the woodland springs—
Thus Daphnis has commanded for his honor.
Then build a tomb and place on the tomb these verses:
'Daphnis was known to these woods and known to the stars;
Lovely the flock, and lovelier still the shepherd.'"

*Menalcas*

Inspired poet, the song you sing is such
As sleep must be to the weary on the grass
Or cool brook water quenching the thirst of summer.
First after him you are, now, fortunate boy,
In singing as in playing worthy your master,
I nevertheless will sing as best I can,
Taking my turn, to raise your Daphnis up

Among the stars; Daphnis shall be high
Among the stars; I too was loved by Daphnis.

*Mopsus*

Nothing could be a greater gift than this;
The boy himself was worthy of your song;
Stimichon long since has praised your singing.

*Menalcas*

"Radiant Daphnis wonders at heaven's threshold,
Seeing the stars and clouds beneath his feet,
And therefore all the countryside, the woods,
And Pan, the Dryads, and the shepherds, too,
Are all of them filled at once with holiday bliss;
No wolf lies down in ambush for the sheep,
No traps are set for the deer. Daphnis loves peace.
The unshorn mountains joyfully shout to the stars,
The groves and rocky places sing together,
'He is a god, Menalcas!' Daphnis, be kind
And bountiful to your own! Behold, I have
Established four altars here: two are for Daphnis,
Two for Apollo. Yearly I will set out
Two bowls of milk, foaming with freshness, and two
Of the richest olive oil, and best of all
For the pleasure of the feast—whether in winter,
Before the fire, or else at the autumn harvest,
Under the shade of trees—I will pour out
Nectareous Ariusian wine from Chios.
Damoetas and Lyctian Aegon will sing for us,

And Alphesiboeus will dance like a leaping satyr.
Thus will it be for you for ever more,
Both at the time of year when it's right to make
Our annual devotions to the Nymphs
And at the time of year when we bless our fields.
As long as the wild boar loves the mountain ridges,
As long as fish love swimming in the rivers,
As long as bees pasture upon the thyme fields,
Cicadas on morning dew, as long as this
The glory of Daphnis will last. Just as, each year,
Farmers make binding vows to Bacchus and Ceres,
So we will make our binding vows to you."

*Mopsus*

What can I give you back for such a song?
It is more beautiful than either the first
Sounds of the South Wind in the early moments
Of Spring beginning, or sounds of waves as they break
Upon the beach, or sounds of mountain streams
Flowing downhill to the valley over stones.

*Menalcas*

First I want to give you this hemlock pipe,
The one on which I learned to play the songs,
"Corydon loved the fair Alexis," and,
"Whose flock is this? Is it Meliboeus' flock?"

*Mopsus*

Here is a beautiful shepherd's staff, the one
Antigenes often asked me for and was

Refused, though then he deserved my love. The knots
Are evenly spaced, the rings are brass, Menalcas.

# Eclogue Nine

Lycidas        Moeris

**Lycidas**

Moeris, why are you taking the path to town?

**Moeris**

O Lycidas, we never thought that what
Has happened to us was ever going to happen,
And now we've lived to see it. A stranger came
To take possession of our farm, and said:
"I own this place; you have to leave this place."
Heartbroken and beaten, since fortune will have it so,
I have to carry these kids to him in town.
I only hope bad luck for him goes with them.

**Lycidas**

But I was told Menalcas with his songs
Had saved the land, from where those hills arise
To where they slope down gently to the water,
Near those old beech trees, with their broken tops.

**Moeris**

Yes, that was the story; but what can music do
Against the weapons of soldiers? When eagles come,
Tell me what doves can possibly do about it?
If the raven on the left in this hollow oak
Hadn't warned me not to resist, I might have been killed.

Menalcas himself might very well have been killed.

*Lycidas*

Oh, how did this calamity befall us?
Alas, the solace that your music brought us,
Was it so nearly lost to us, Menalcas?
Who else would sing of the Nymphs? And who would scatter
The wildflowers on the ground or shade the springs
With the green shade of trees? And who would sing
Such songs as the one I overheard one day
That you were singing as you were setting off
To visit Amaryllis, our delight:
"Tityrus, while I'm gone, please feed my goats
(I won't be gone for long) and when you've fed them,
Please drive them down to the water, and when you do,
Be careful of the billy-goat; he butts."

*Moeris*

Yes, and then that poem, addressed to Varus,
Though not completed as yet: "Varus, your name—
If Mantua can be spared, our Mantua,
Alas, too close to woeful Cremona—the swans,
Singing, will carry your name up to the stars."

*Lycidas*

So that your cows may feast on clover grass,
That makes their udders prosper and be more ample,
And so that your bees may avoid the Corsican yews,
If you have any song to sing, begin.
The Pierian maidens have made me a poet too,
For I have songs; the shepherds call me a poet;
But I don't really believe them, at least not yet.
Nothing I've sung so far is good enough

For Varius or Cinna to listen to.
My songs are honking geese among the swans.

*Moeris*

Lycidas, I have been saying the words of a song,
Over and over, trying to bring them back . . .
It's a good old song . . . "O Galatea, come . . .
O come away to me. Come from the sea . . .
What pleasure is there, there? . . . The spring is here . . .
Earth scatters her many varied flowers here . . . ,
And here the poplar leans above the grotto . . .
Where grapevine tendrils laced create a shade . . .
O let the waves crash raging on the shore."

*Lycidas*

What was that song I heard you singing, alone,
The other night, under a cloudless sky?
I'd remember the tune . . . if I could remember the words . . .
" . . . Daphnis . . . tell me . . . why are you gazing only
At those old constellations in the sky? . . .
Look, Venus's grandson's Caesar's star is rising . . .
The star that brings such joy to the ripening grain . . .
And deepens the colors of grapes on the sunny vines.
. . . Daphnis, plant your pear trees . . . years from now
The children of your children will gather the pears. . . ."

*Moeris*

Time takes all we have away from us;
I remember when I was a boy I used to sing
Every long day of summer down to darkness,
And now I am forgetting all my songs;

My voice grows hoarse; I must have been seen by a wolf.
Menalcas will sing the songs for you, when he comes.

*Lycidas*

The more you put me off the more I long
To hear the songs. See, how for you the waves
Make themselves quiet as they come in to shore.
The murmuring of the breeze is utterly stilled.
We're halfway on our journey to the town;
The sepulchre of Bianor is just ahead;
See where the laborers there have pruned the trees.
Moeris, let's stop here and sing our songs.
Put down the baby goats; we'll make it to town;
Or if you're afraid it's going to rain tonight,
Let's keep on going, but singing as we go.
Singing makes the journey easier.
I'll carry the basket awhile, so you can sing.

*Moeris*

No more of that; let's just go on our way.
The time for singing will be when Menalcas comes.

TWO EPISTLES OF HORACE

# Epistle ii. 2

*To Florus*


    Florus, dear friend, suppose somebody offered
To sell you a slave, and made the following sales talk:
"A good looking boy; the asking price 8,000;
Born in Italy; very willing and able;
He reads a little Greek; he's a very quick learner;
He's malleable, you can make of him what you will;
At drink time he can sing you a song or two,
Pleasingly if somewhat artlessly.
Believe you me, when a salesman like me is under
Pressure to make a sale and anxiously makes
Too many promises, why then of course he loses
The customer's trust. But *I'm* under no such pressure.
I have no debts. None of the other dealers
Is able to make you such an offer as this,
Nor would I make it to just anyone.
I'll tell you this: there was one time when the boy
Ran off, in a truant way, and hid himself
Under the stairs, because he was scared of a whipping.
If you're not bothered by this peccadillo
I've told you about, give me the price I ask."

I think the salesman who handled the sale this way
Would make the sale and get his price, without worry.
If the customer had bought with his eyes open,
He'd know what the fault had been. If it happened again,
Wouldn't it be unjust to sue the salesman?
I told you when you were leaving, how lazy I am,
A couch potato. I told you so you wouldn't
Scold me for never answering your letters.
What was the point of telling you this if you
Still scold me, not only about the letters
But about the unsent poems I promised to send.

    Once upon a time in Lucullus's army
There was a soldier who by working hard
Had saved a lot of money, but then, one night,
All of it was stolen. Gnashing his teeth
Like a starving wolf, furious at himself
And furious at whoever it was who stole it,
He single-handedly drove out a royal
Garrison from a fortified position
Where there was stored an awful lot of riches.
Glory he won and more than 20,000
Sesterces in reward for this exploit.
A short time after this his captain wanted
To attack another fort, and, using terms
That might have stirred up courage in the heart
Of even the timidest of men, he said,
"Go where your valor tells you to go, stout heart!
Good fortune come to you! Win the rewards
Your deeds deserve!—Why are you standing still?"
To which the rustic fellow said, "Why don't you
Tell it to somebody who's just lost his money."

I got my schooling in Rome and learned about
How bad Achilles' anger was for the Greeks,
And then of course I went on to Athens to study
Eagerly under those Academic trees
The nature of truth and how to tell crooked from straight.
And then the hard times came, and I was taken,
A raw recruit, away from that pleasant grove
And swept by the tide of war onto the field,
Among the others fighting with weapons useless
Against the powerful arms of Caesar Augustus.
Philippi happened and so I was discharged,
But my wings were clipped, and I was stripped of money
And stripped of my father's property. And so
It was because of poverty that I
Was forced to write my verses. But now that I'm
Pretty well off, what drug do you think I'd take
To make me think it better to write than sleep?

The years as they go by take everything with them,
One thing after another; they've taken away
Laughter, and revelry, and love from me, and now
They want to take poetry. What can I do?
Not everybody's the same in matters of taste.
You like my songs; another likes my epodes;
Another of you likes my caustic satires.
It seems to me it's as if three guests for dinner
Had likes and dislikes in food that were all at odds.
So what should I serve up? What should I not?
For you'd send back to the kitchen what one of them ordered,
And what you like disgusts the other two.

And anyway, what makes you think that I
Can write in Rome, with all I have to do there?

First this one wants a letter of introduction;
Then that one wants me to put aside everything
And listen to what he's written only this morning;
Then somebody else, who lives on the Quirinal,
Is sick in bed, and so is somebody else,
Who lives way off on the back of the Aventine,
And I'm supposed to sick room visit both.

     "Well, but the streets are quiet, so you'll be able
To think about your poems on your way over."

     Oh, sure. Tell me about it. First there'll be
A contractor with his gear and all his workmen,
And then a giant crane in the way, first hoisting
A great huge stone and then a great huge log,
And then here comes a funeral procession
Jostling its way along through all the traffic
Of great huge rattling wagons, and all of a sudden
A mad dog runs by one way through the street
And a filthy runaway pig the other way.
"Work on writing sonorous verses enroute"?
The choir of poets loves groves and hates the city,
Faithful to Bacchus, who loves to sleep in the shade.
Do you really want me to follow the path of art
Amid all the noise that goes on all day and all night?
An artist who's made the choice to live in Athens,
A quiet place like that, even there, when he
Comes out of his study and walks about the town,
He's tongue-tied as a statue, an object of laughter.
In Rome, in the social hubbub, do you suppose
That I'd be able to put together the words
That would awaken the music of the lyre?

There were two brothers in Rome, one was a lawyer,
The other an orator, and all day long
All you could hear were the praises of each for the other.
If one of them was a Gracchus to the other,
The other one was a Mucius to his brother.
It's just like that with our nest of singing bards.
I write an ode; my friend an elegy:
"Oh, marvelous! You're blessed by all nine Muses!"
If you could see with what complacency
We stand in that room in the Library of Apollo
Companionably eying the medallions
Of famous dead authors there, and then if you
Drew near and listened to how we talk to each other,
You'd find out how our ivy crowns get woven.
Like Samnite fighters in an endless battle
We bash each other with compliments as we go at it.
He says to me, You're exactly like Alcaeus!
And according to me, he is? —Callimachus.
And if he seems to need more, then he's Mimnermus,
And so he gets the title that he wants.
I used to go out of my way to soothe the nerves
Of anxious touchy writers, when I myself
Was writing and touchy and anxiously seeking approval,
But now that that's all over, now that I'm back
In my right mind, I'd gladly stop up my ears
When anyone threatens to read me what he's just written.
The people who write bad poetry are a joke,
But writing makes them happy and it makes them
Happily reverential of themselves.
If they hear no praise from you, what do they care?
Deaf to your silence they'll praise themselves, serenely.

But he who desires to write a legitimate poem
Will be an honest critic of what he does.
He won't be afraid, if some expression doesn't
Seem right, if it lacks the appropriate weight
Or lustre, or's wrong for the tone of the passage it's part of,
To take it away, although it's reluctant to go
And struggles to keep the place it felt enshrined in.
He'll dig up obscure old words such as Cato used,
Or Cethegus used, and bring them back, from where
They'd languished in the dark of the long ago,
Into the light of day, alive with meaning.
He'll be willing to use new words in poetry,
Made valid by their valid use by men
Going about their daily work or play.
Steady, flowing, pure, just as a river
Is steady, flowing, and pure, he will pour forth
Power, and bless his country with a rich language.
He'll prune back what is overgrown,
Smooth out what's rough, get rid of whatever weakness
Inhibits power; he'll make it look like child's play,
Although, in fact, he tortures himself to do so;
His dancing moves with grace, like a satyr, now,
And now the way an oafish Cyclops moves.

I think I'd just as soon be thought to be
A silly and incompetent hack, so long
As I was perfectly happy with my faults
Or perfectly unaware of them, rather than be
Grinding my teeth to endure my own self-knowledge.
Once there was at Argos a well-regarded
Citizen whose mind was taken over
By the fantasy that he was sitting alone,
A privileged audience of one, in a theater,

Enthusiastically applauding as he listened
To a marvelous company of tragic actors
Performing just for him. This citizen
In every other way was entirely normal:
He never had any trouble with the neighbors;
He was a genial host, and kind to his wife;
If one of his servants happened to break a jar,
He didn't go crazy, he wasn't that kind of master.
In short, this man was the sort of person who wasn't
Likely to fall down a well or over a cliff.
His relatives worried about his fantasy
And got him cured with a dose of hellebore,
But when he was cured and back in his senses he told them,
"You think you've cured me but actually you've killed me.
The illusion you took away was what I lived on."

     Certainly it's right to put away
All childish things and leave to children such games
As trying to find exactly the proper words
To calibrate to the cadences and meter
Of the Latin lyre, and right to study instead
The cadences and meter of living right.
That's why, over and over, I find myself
Thinking about things in the following ways:
Suppose you had a thirst that nothing would quench;
The more water you drank, the more you wanted.
You'd go to a doctor. And if the richer you get,
The richer you need to be, isn't there someone
You need to consult? Suppose you had a sore
And the herbs the doctor prescribed weren't able to cure it,
Wouldn't you give up using the herbs he prescribed?
Maybe somebody told you that the richer
You got to be with possessions the gods had given,

The freer you'd be from being possessed by folly;
Now that you're richer, you know, you're not a bit wiser.
Maybe it's time to listen to somebody else.
If money could give you wisdom and free you from folly
And make you independent of anxiety,
Then surely you'd be abashed if there was anyone
Anywhere in the world more greedy than you.

       Of course it's true that you're the owner of what
You've paid for with a lot of money and
Deeds signed, and all of that. But if you listen
To what they say who are learned in the law,
Use is a kind of ownership as well.
In a sense you own the farm whose produce feeds you;
You're the master of the farmer who plows the land
Preparing it for the corn you're going to buy.
You pay some money, and you own some eggs,
A chicken, some grapes, maybe some wine, and so,
Little by little you're buying the farm that someone
Once paid three hundred thousand sesterces or more for.
What difference whether the payment was now or then?
The man who's bought a farm at Veii or Aricia
Has only bought, no matter what he thinks,
The salad for his dinner, the logs for the fire
To heat the kettle on, of a chilly evening.
His view of the matter is of course that he owns
The whole kit and kaboodle, out to where
The poplars are planted to mark the boundary clearly,
To head off possible neighborly disputes.
Imagine somebody thinking he's the owner,
When what he thinks he owns so easily passes
Into the hands of somebody else, say by

Foreclosure or by eminent domain,
Or if no other way, at the last, by death.

So if nobody has the use of anything
In perpetuity, and therefore if
Heir follows heir as one wave follows another,
What is the use of storehouses full of grain
From your vast estate, or vast extents of forests
In Lucania, and others in Calabria,
If Death, who can't be tempted by your money,
Gathers the rich man in along with the poor.

Jewels, marble, ivory, paintings, beautiful Tuscan
Pottery, silver, Gaetulian robes dyed purple—
Many there are who'd love to have all of these things.
There are some who don't care about them in the least.
Why one twin brother lives for nothing but pleasure,
And loves to fool around even more than Herod
Loves his abundant gardens of date-trees, while
The other twin brother works from morning to night
Improving his farm, plowing and clearing the lands,
Pruning and planting, working his ass off, only
The Genius knows, the personal god who knows
And controls the birth star of every person
There is in the world. The personal god, the god
Who dies in a sense when your own breath gives out,
And yet lives on after you die to be
The personal god of somebody other than you,
Your personal god whose countenance changes as
He looks at you, smiling sometimes, sometimes not.

I'll do the best I can with what I have,
And I'm not going to worry about whatever

My heir might think because I've left so little.
But at the same time I want to be sure I know
The difference there is between the spendthrift and
The man who's open-hearted and generous,
And also the difference there is between the man
Who's prudent because he knows the value of things
And the miser who simply can't let anything go.
There *is* a distinction between just wantonly
Throwing your money away in a prodigal fashion
And being perfectly willing to spend and not
Unduly concerned with holding onto it all,
Seizing the chance for pleasure when it comes,
Like a schoolboy let out of school at holiday time.
Keep direst poverty far away from me;
But other than that, whether the ship be large
Or be it small that I'm a passenger on,
I'm still the same passenger, always one and the same,
Not always sped full sail by a favoring wind
And yet not always laboring through a storm,
Always more or less what I was before,
In my person and place in life somewhere behind
Those who are first, somewhere ahead of the last.

You're not avaricious? Fine. But, tell me, did
All other frailties go away when that did?
Are you free in your heart from hungry ambition, say?
Are you scared to death by the very thought of death?
Are you able to laugh at dreams, or the spooks of magic?
At wizards? Ghosts? Things that go whoosh in the night?
Thessalian wizards' omens? Do you count with relief
Every new birthday you've managed to make it through?
Do you always forgive the faults you see in your friends?
Are you getting any better as you get older?

Are you any kinder than you used to be?
What have you gained if you've plucked out just one thorn,
When you've got so many others in your foot?
If you haven't learned yet how to live right, well, then,
Get out of the way of others who might learn better.
You've played enough, you've eaten and drunk enough;
Maybe it's time to say goodbye, before
You've had too much to drink and get made fun of
And elbowed out by younger people who know
Better than you do how to have fun at the party.

# Envoi

## Epistle i.13

*To Vinnius Asina*

Just as I've told you over and over, Vinny,
Deliver these books of mine to Augustus only
If you know for sure that he's in good health and only
If you know for sure that he's in a good mood and only
If it comes about that he asks in person to see it.
I'm worried you'll be so eager to help me you'll botch it,
And I'll be a figure of fun because of you.
If the bagful of books annoys you by being too heavy,
Throw it away, anything rather than bring it
Into his presence and plop it resentfully down,
Turning your patronymic, Asina, into
A joke that everyone there has a good laugh at.

Struggle manfully on, making your way
Over mountains and rivers and swamps, through snow and sleet;
Be careful about how you carry it, not, for example,
Under your armpit, the way some hayseed carries
A lamb to market, or as a drunken housemaid
Tries to conceal a ball of wool she stole,
Or a poor man invited to dinner by some rich cousin
Carries his felt hat and sandals, not knowing what else
To do. And Vinny, please, when you get there,

Don't tell whoever you meet what it cost you in sweat
To carry this bag of poems all the way there,
These poems of mine that might just possibly catch
The attention of Caesar's eyes and Caesar's ears.

Go on, keep on, no matter who tries to stop you.
Go on. Farewell. Be careful, Vinny. Watch out.
Through heat and cold and dark of night, don't stumble.
Handle with care this precious package of mine.

# Notes

Cover illustration: Detail from a Roman mosaic representing the Epicurean philosophy.

NEW POEMS AND TRANSLATIONS

Dedicatory poem: from Rossell Hope Robbins, ed., Secular Lyrics of the XIVth and XVth Centuries (Oxford: Clarendon Press, 1952), pp. 130f.

"Wolf Woman": Based on a case cited in Harvey A. Rosenstock and Kenneth B. Vincent, "A Case of Lycanthropy," A Lycanthropy Reader, edited by Charlotte F. Otten (Syracuse, NY: Syracuse University Press, 1986).

"Song of the Drunkard": Rainer Maria Rilke, Das Buch der Bilde (Berlin: Juncker, 1906).

"On a Poem by Arthur R. Gold": The poem is one of "Three Fragments: Things That Last," Poems Written During a Period of Sickness (Somerville, MA: Firefly Press, 1989). Reprinted by permission.

"Wallenda": The concluding lines are quoted from an article in Newsweek, 3 April 1978.

"My Harvest": The translation is taken from the first two stanzas of Hölderlin's "Mein Eigentum," the German text of which is in Michael Hamburger, ed., Hymns and Fragments (Cambridge: Cambridge University Press, 1966).

"Hälfte des Lebens": The translation is of the German text in Hymns and Fragments (Michael Hamburger, ed. [Cambridge: 1966]).

"An die Parzen": The translation is of the German text in Hymns and Fragments, as cited above.

"News from Mount Amiata": A translation of "Notizie dall'Amiata" by Eugenio Montale, from Le Occasioni, in Poesie (Milan: Mondadori 1939).

"She Speaks Across the Years": A translation of "Wenn Aus der Ferne...," the German text in Hymns and Fragments, as cited above.

"Roman Elegy X": A translation of the German text in L. R. Lind, Johann Wolfgang von

*Goethe's Roman Elegies and Venetian Epigrams: A Bilingual Text* (Wichita: University Press of Kansas, 1974).

*"That Evening at Dinner"*: A number of quotations are based on *The American Heritage Dictionary* (Boston: Houghton Mifflin, 1992). The quotations from Doctor Johnson are taken from his review of Soame Jenyn's *A Free Inquiry into the Nature and Origin of Evil* (1759), in *Rasselas, Poems and Selected Prose,* edited by Bertrand Bronson (New York: Holt Rinehart and Winston, 1971), and essay #78 in Johnson's journal *The Rambler,* in *The Yale Edition of the Works of Samuel Johnson* (New Haven: Yale University Press, 1969), IV, edited by W. J. Bate and Albrecht B. Strauss.

*"Shubshi-meshre-Shakkan"*: A rendering based on the translation by W. G. Lambert, in *Ancient Near Eastern Texts Relating to the Old Testament,* 3d ed., edited by James B. Pritchard (Princeton: Princeton University Press, 1969).

*"First Night"*: The Latin phrase, *Timor mortis conturbat me,* translates as "the fear of death dismays me" and is from William Dunbar's (1460?–1520?) "Lament for the Makers."


STRANGERS: A BOOK OF POEMS


*Epigraph:* The epigraph is quoted from *Two Elizabethan Puritan Diaries,* edited by Marshall N. Knappen (Chicago: American Society of Church History, 1933), p. 103.

*"Sculptures by Dimitri Hadzi"*: In reprisal for the killing of thirty-two German soldiers by the *Resistenza* in Rome, the Germans gathered together 335 Romans, representing all classes, ages, and occupations, and slaughtered them in the Ardeatine Caves on 24 March 1944.

*"Caprimulgidae"*: Information and some phraseology are taken from several ornithological books, most particularly from John Gooders, *The Great Book of Birds* (New York: Dial, 1975).

*"Out at Lanesville"*: "Their lives have separate ends" is a quotation from Longfellow's great poem "The Fire of Driftwood."

*"At the Hospital"*: ("As with the soft authority of wings") was originally published in *Dwelling Places.* I have moved it back to its proper place in this earlier book.

*"After Spotsylvania Court House"*: The battle took place between May 8 and 11, 1864. "A Charge to Keep" is no. 388 in *The Methodist Hymnal.* The quotations in this poem are from a letter of Joseph H. Knowles to his wife, Ellin J. Knowles, 23 May 1864.

*"Photographs from a Book: Six Poems"*: Several of the photographs evoked in the poems

are related to photographs reproduced in *The Photographs of Thomas Eakins,* edited by Gordon Hendricks (New York: Grossman, 1972).

The quotations in poems iv and vi are from notes to photographs in this book.

The quotation in poem ii is from Ovid, *Fasti,* 2.289ff, as translated in Erwin Panofsky, *Meaning in the Visual Arts* (New York: Doubleday, 1955), p. 299.

The quotation in poem iii, lines 13–14, is from Ovid, *Metamorphoses* 9.371–73.

The Anasazi, referred to in poem v, line 1, are the Old People, prehistoric Indians of the Southwest.

The quotation in poem v, lines 7–9, is paraphrased from the article on Photography in *The World Book Encyclopedia* (1966 edition), 15: 380.

*"Counterpart":* The quotation in lines 8–13 is from an obituary article on Joseph H. Knowles in a Methodist journal from 1898. Lines 26–28: these and similar verses are found on the so-called Orphic Gold Leaf fragments. See Gunther Zuntz, *Persephone* (New York: Oxford University Press, 1971), pp. 277–93, and Emily Vermeule, *Aspects of Death in Early Greek Art and Poetry* (Berkeley: University of California Press, 1979), p. 58.

Lebadeia is the place of an oracle, near the sources of the rivers Lethe and Mnemosyne.


DWELLING PLACES: POEMS AND TRANSLATIONS


In cases where a poem in this book derives from another poem or prose passage I have simply cited under the title the name of the author or other source. I have not tried to differentiate between attempts at relatively close translations, freer renderings, and adaptations.

I am greatly indebted to Rodney Dennis, Rodney Lister, William L. Moran, and Lawrence Rosenwald, among others, for translation suggestions and for active help in these matters. I have a general indebtedness also to Richard Bernheimer, *Wild Men in the Middle Ages* (New York: Octagon, 1979) and Timothy Husband, *The Wild Man: Medieval Myth and Symbolism* (New York: Metropolitan Museum of Art, 1980).

*"Harvesters Resting":* The title is the title of a painting by Millet in the Museum of Fine Arts, Boston.

*"The Lesson":* Adapted from the Latin poem of Samuel Johnson, *"Errat adhuc vitreus per prata virentia rivus,"* in *Works,* VI (New Haven: Yale University Press, 1964), edited by E. L. McAdam, Jr., with George Milne. I am indebted to the prose translation in this volume.

"*Abyss*": "*Le Gouffre,*" in *Fleurs du Mal.*

"*Autumn*": "*Herbst,*" in *Das Buch der Bilder.*

"*Herbsttag*": In *Das Buch der Bilder.*

"*When We Were Children*": The original can be found in *German and Italian Lyrics of the Middle Ages,* edited by Frederick Goldin (New York: Anchor, 1972).

"*Unos Caballos*": *Cántico: A Selection,* edited by Norman Thomas Giovanni (Boston: Little, Brown, 1965).

"*Levis Exsurgit Zephirus*": See Peter Dronke, *The Medieval Lyric* (Cambridge: Cambridge University Press, 1977), pp. 92–94.

"*Of Violets*": *An Anthology of Neo-Latin Poetry,* edited by Fred J. Nichols (New Haven: Yale University Press, 1979). I am indebted to the prose translation in this volume.

"*Roman Elegy VIII*": German text from *Johann Wolfgang von Goethe's Roman Elegies and Venetian Epigrams: A Bilingual Text* (Wichita: University Press of Kansas, 1974).

"*Strabo Reading Megasthenes*": Strabo, *Geography,* 15.I.57 (edited by Leonard Jones [London, 1930, VII, 95 (Loeb Classical Library)]).

"*Civilization and Its Discontents*": See Sigmund Freud, *Civilization and Its Discontents,* Chapter II; Anne Claude Phillipe, "*Comte de Caylus, Vie de Watteau,*" in *Vies des Artistes du XVIIIième Siècle; Discours sur la Peinture et la Sculpture,* edited by A. Fontaine (Paris, 1910). There is a translation in Edmond and Jules de Goncourt, *French XVIII Century Painters,* edited by Robin Ironside (London: Phaidon, 1948). The painting is in the National Gallery of Scotland, Edinburgh.

"*Mnemosyne*": Based mainly on the first version of this poem by Hölderlin, with some use also of the third version. I am especially indebted here to Rodney Dennis and Lawrence Rosenwald, and to Michael Hamburger, translator of *Poems and Fragments* (Cambridge, UK: Cambridge University Press, 1966), and to *Hymns and Fragments by Friedrich Hölderlin,* translated by Richard Sieburth (Princeton: Princeton University Press, 1984).

"*Prayer to the Gods of the Night*": This is based on the literal translation from the Old Babylonian by William L. Moran.

GILGAMESH: A NEW RENDERING IN ENGLISH VERSE

I should explain the constraints within which I have worked. I cannot read cuneiform and do not know the language, or languages, the Gilgamesh epic was written in. As my sources and authorities I have used three literal line-by-line translations, first and foremost "The Epic of Gilgamesh," by E. A. Speiser in *Ancient Near Eastern*

*Texts Relating to the Old Testament* (Princeton: Princeton University Press, 1969), and two more recent works, *Gilgamesh,* by John Gardner and John Maier (New York: Vintage, 1985) and *The Epic of Gilgamesh,* by Maureen Gallery Kovacs (Stanford, CA: Stanford University Press, 1989). I have also consulted the excellent prose free version by N. K. Sandars, *The Epic of Gilgamesh* (New York: Penguin, 1972), based on Sumerian as well as Akkadian originals.

Gilgamesh, King of Uruk, and his companion the Wild Man Enkidu have offended the gods by their heroic deeds, first by killing Huwawa the Demon Guardian of the Cedar Forest and then by killing the Bull of Heaven sent down to punish them at the behest of the goddess Ishtar, whose sexual advances Gilgamesh had rejected. The gods decided that one of them must die and Enkidu was chosen.

Enlil is the god of order, comparable in some ways with Zeus. Anu is the god of the sea. Shamash is the sun god.

The hunter, in Tablet I, saw Enkidu with the wild animals at the watering places and saw him unsetting his traps. The hunter complained to Gilgamesh, who sent Shamhat the temple prostitute to have sexual intercourse with Enkidu and so make him more fully human. Enkidu then went to Uruk and fought with Gilgamesh, who defeated him. After this they became friends and set out on their exploits.

Etana was an early Sumerian king. Sumuqan is god of cattle.


THE ODES OF HORACE: A TRANSLATION


*"To Leuconoë":* Ouija board is a modern substitution for Babylonian numbers, *"Babylonios . . . numeros."*

*"To Varus":* In some respects, this is more freely translated than most of the others. Obviously, there's no bartop in the Latin.

*"To the Republic":* "your onboard gods," refers to images of household gods carried onboard the ship for good luck.

*"Of Cleopatra":* The occasion of the poem is news of the final defeat and deaths of Antony and Cleopatra (30 BCE).

*"Of the God's Power":* Atlas (of the Atlas mountain range) was a Titan, a son of Zeus and Maia.

Taenarus is a cape on the southern coast of the Peloponnesus and regarded as a location of an entrance to the Underworld.

*"To Tyndaris":* Faunus is a god of the country, of agriculture, and of rural festivity, and a protector of poets; he is the Roman god closest to Pan in his attributes.

*"To His Lyre"*: There has been disagreement, based on manuscript discrepancies, about whether the first phrase of the Latin is *Poscimus* or *Poscimur*. Some translators therefore read the opening phrase as "We are" (or "I am") asked for a song. I've chosen the other reading because it seems more appropriate for the prayer that is the poem.

THE ECLOGUES OF VIRGIL: A TRANSLATION

*"Eclogue Five"*:
This poem derives from Theocritus, *Idyls* 1, 6 and 7.
**thyrsus:** The staff Bacchus carries.
**Pales:** Goddess of pastures and herds.
**Dryads:** Wood-nymphs.
**Chios:** A Greek island in the Aegean. The best wines came from there, and the very best came from a region of the island called Ariusia.
**Lyctian:** Cretan.
**"Corydon loved the fair Alexis"**: Quotes the first line of Eclogue ii.
**"Whose flock is this? Is it Meliboeus' flock?"**: Quotes the first line of Eclogue iii.
**Antigenes:** The name comes from Theocritus, *Idyl* 7.

*"Eclogue Nine"*:
**"I own this place. . . ."**: Moeris has been dispossessed of his ownership of his land, probably because the ownership has been given to a discharged veteran of Augustus's army.
**Varus:** P. Alfenus Varus, consul, and a general. He was one of Augustus's three administrators charged with the redistribution of property that Meliboeus, in Eclogue i, and Moeris, in Eclogue ix, and, apparently, Virgil's family, suffered from.
**Mantua:** The town near which Virgil was born.
**Cremona:** A town in the Po Valley which had suffered egregiously from Augustus's redistribution of land.
**" . . . so that your bees may avoid Corsican yews"**: Corsica was famous for inferior honey.
**Pierian maidens:** The Muses.
**Varius:** Varius Rufus, Virgil's friend and literary executor, a poet whom Virgil and Horace greatly admired. His works are lost.
**Cinna:** A poet admired by Virgil; he was a friend of Catullus.

**Venus's grandson Caesar's star:** A comet that appeared shortly after Julius Caesar's assassination.

**Bianor:** Another herdsman.

TWO EPISTLES OF HORACE

*"Epistle ii.2":*
**Florus:** Julius Florus, a young poet, writer of satires.
**Gracchus and Mucius:** Roman statesmen celebrated for virtue.
**Alcaeus, Callimachus, Mimnermus:** celebrated Greek poets.

*"Epistle i.13":* Vinnius's father's cognomen was Asina, which means "donkey."

2289; 8164; 347 ... 7 7 435

8/8/7/ ... (

1, 174, 325
+ 20
285  1305

6, 174, 020

6, 991

1305 + 20
285

97, 296

God Goddess, Grandmother

3; 637; 7476; 6297, 703     6/12